Home,
My Story of House
and Personal Restoration
A Memoir

D1662731

M.G. Barlow

Wherever you go, may you always be home

Black Rose Writing | Texas

This is a book of non-fiction, and all of the events, dates, and people are described to the best of the author's recollection. Some of the names have been changed to protect the privacy of individuals mentioned.

ISBN: 978-1-68433-776-7
PUBLISHED BY BLACK ROSE WRITING
www.blackrosewriting.com

Printed in the United States of America
Suggested Retail Price (SRP) $18.95

Home, My Story of House and Personal Restoration is printed in Sabon.

*As a planet-friendly publisher, Black Rose Writing does its best to eliminate unnecessary waste to reduce paper usage and energy costs, while never compromising the reading experience. As a result, the final word count vs. page count may not meet common expectations.

Author photo on back cover by Glenn Livermore Photography, Newburyport, MA

Watercolor painting in middle of the book by Sue Dion, Uxbridge MA

To my sons, Geoff and Greg, for enriching my spirit, helping me grow, and keeping me home.

Home,
My Story of House
and Personal Restoration

sympathy   materie   Herz

"To us, our house was not insentient matter—it had a heart and a soul and eyes to see us with, and approvals and solicitudes and
tief deep sympathies; it was of us, and we were in its confidence, and
lived in its grace and in the peace of its benediction. We never
came home from an absence that its face did not light up and
speak out its eloquent welcome—and we could not enter it
unmoved." ungerührt Fehlen   eingeben

—Mark Twain in a letter to his friend Joseph Twichell

eintragen

Anmut   stück   Segnung

Chapter 1

When I was seven, I took a nap in my own bed and woke up in a strange house. Oh, it was the same big, old place I'd grown up in. A white New Englander in Chelmsford, Massachusetts, a suburb of Boston where neighbors act proud and private. Barely in Chelmsford, that is. The place stood on the edge of town, the second-to-last street before crossing over into the mill city, Lowell. During my slumber that day, our home changed so much it felt like awakening to a foster family in another state.

"Mary Gayle, are you there?" Uncle Johnny called from outside my bedroom door. Dad's brother never came upstairs. His voice broke, as if laughing and unable to get all the words out. I opened the door. Uncle Johnny's cheeks were wet. His eyes, red.

"We are going to Vovô and Vovó's," he said. (Pronounced "va-voo" and "va-vore," these mean grandfather and grandmother in Portuguese.) In silence, I followed this thin man I'd known all my young life downstairs, into the den, and over our red-white-red tiles. The worn wooden door howled to the fresh air. We walked past Ma's Virgin Mary statue and under my brother Michael's weeping willow, along a little dirt path in the grass between our house and the one Dad grew up in.

Michael, a skinny, blond nine-year-old, sat there at our grandparents' Formica table playing checkers against Auntie Celia's boyfriend—who invited me to play the winner. We took turns playing checkers until day eased into night. Michael never mentioned how he'd found Ma that day. In fact, for the rest of his life, he and I never discussed it.

Vovô (va-voo), wearing suspenders over a white t-shirt, usually smiled. Often teased me by tapping the back of my leg with his cane. Vovó (va-vore) wore a full-length peasant dress and long apron. She kept her gray hair in a low tight bun. Usually gave me wet kisses on the cheek and brought my little brother, Donnie, salty cabbage soup with kidney beans and ham. This day, though, Vovô and Vovó shuffled into the kitchen, observed us, then drifted out—like ghosts. After dark, a teenage cousin arrived.

"They want them home now," she said.

So we followed her along the little dirt path in the grass back to our house. Since I'd left that afternoon with Uncle Johnny, our driveway filled up with cars. All our windows glowed yellow. The wooden door shrieked open, plunging us into a chorus of wailing, sniffling, and nose blowing. Many, many grownups stepped aside, making a narrow way for us across our red-white-red kitchen floor and into the den straight to Dad—Dad with his steel wool hair. He sat on a tattered green leather office seat, the one Ma used as she oscillated on roller wheels between her billing desk and sewing machine. His eyes were glassy and bloodshot. I had never seen the guy cry before. Dad brought a crumpled handkerchief to his eyes and dragged the cloth back and forth against his nostrils.

Michael looked at our father and asked, "Is she?"

Through his sobs, Dad replied, "Yes."

No one explained to me Ma died this day. I just knew. I didn't ask how. Relatives snatched Michael off in one direction, me in another.

Someone placed me on our lumpy green sofa among many aunties—Dad's sisters and sisters-in-law. I asked a litany of questions. "Who will help me get ready for school? Who will make my breakfast?" and on and on. The aunties took turns extinguishing each inquiry.

"I will come in the morning and help you get ready for school," Auntie Theresa said.

"I can make sure you get your breakfast," Auntie Celia said.

"You can come stay with Donna and me if you want," Auntie Viola said, referring to my cousin, Donna, who had a couple of years on me.

2

Their efforts to calm my hysteria conveyed they thought my situation no more pressing than losing a favorite dollie. Exhausted by the back and forth, I stopped asking questions. I cried.

Other aunties poured into the room—Ma's sisters. Auntie Edna fainted. Uncles—three uncles maybe?—gathered about her, eased her into a chair. A recliner? Uncle Johnny wafted something under her nose. She awoke. She howled.

An auntie escorted me to the kitchen where my twenty-three-year-old sister, Dorothea, stood against our stove. Crying, she held her lowered head in one hand and a tissue in the other. She put an arm around my shoulders and drew me near. Big sister. Little sister. We said nothing. We cried.

Before everything went wrong, that old house embodied a child's wonderland for Michael and me. The floor grate was my favorite feature. Embedded in the floor between the upstairs and the downstairs, its fancy black iron was round and about the size of a bread dish. Like watching a vintage film, I see Michael and myself, a chubby little brunette, as children kneeling in our footed pajamas upstairs around the grate, spying through its curlicues on grownups watching late-night television in our living room below.

Looking down, I observed Dorothea. A slender frame, blond hair. Face as flawless as an angel's. She wore a light crewneck sweater over slacks. Her fingers busily cast yarn on and off needles as she swayed backwards and forwards in a rocking chair. Ma, at one end of our green sofa, also knitted. She wore her "house dress," a knee-length plaid cotton dress buttoned all the way up. Ma's ankles rested one crossed over another, bulging from her black oxfords. Ma's legs depicted a complex topography of thick blue varicose veins.

Opposite the television, Dad, still wearing his green work uniform, slept with his head tilted back on his cushioned chair. A few strands of Dad's steel wool hair laid across a bald spot on top—something Dad boasted about by saying, "Grass don't grow on busy streets."

When his eyes opened, we'd witness the color of a New England sky on a clear spring day.

A Jesus figurine cloaked in turquoise satin stood on a shelf above the television, arms out, palms up as if inviting us all to pray with him. We'd soon need praying for.

From our perch by the grate, I strained for words from low undertones of Ma and Dorothea's conversation. Perhaps they discussed the television program or maybe wedding plans. Dorothea had ordered invitations. Scheduled her wedding for later that year—in August 1968.

"Two-four-seven to Nine-one-three," a female dispatcher shouted at a patrolman through Dad's police scanner. *Static.* "Head over to Route 3 rest area, north bound lane. Got a report of a guy exposing himself in his car. It's a black Corvette. The caller didn't get a plate number."

Dad owned a towing and car repair shop. Through his scanner, he hoped to get a head start on car accidents and breakdowns. This long black radio sat atop our refrigerator amid Hershey's bars and bananas and dust. Even when Dad wasn't home, the scanner droned on. Besides car troubles, our town's robberies, assault and batteries, and suspicious people came into our home day and night through the scanner.

"Two-four-seven to Nine-one-four," a female dispatcher shouted to a patrolman. *Static.* "Head over to Manning Road. A woman says her drunk husband's threatening to kick the door down."

Hovering over the floor grate, Michael and I locked eyes and pursed our lips to prevent inevitable explosions of laughter, rejoicing in our stealthy behavior.

My big brother Jackie walked into the room below, belting out one of his usual chants, "Ice cream! You scream! We all scream for ice cream!"

A burly man, even at about twenty, he wore a dull white t-shirt and green work pants. He and Ma exchanged hellos as he sat on the couch beside her, opposite Dorothea.

"Dor," he said, as he nodded a greeting toward my sister. She looked up at him and said nothing while counting rows of the sweater growing on her lap.

My lips gave way. A snicker escaped as I managed retaining gales of laughter wanting to fly out, too. The grownups, except Dad, who continued snoozing, scowled up at the grate.

"You better git back in bed before I come up there and beat the livin' daylights outta ya," Jackie said, hammering a finger through the air at us.

We scurried away giggling.

"Nine-one-four to Two-four-seven," a patrolman blared out to the female dispatcher. *Static.* "We just stopped by. The wife said he left. She doesn't wanna file a restraining order. We're heading back to the station." *Static.*

Built around 1900, our house was one of us. It witnessed our troubles and kept our secrets. Our moods reflected on its walls, commiserating with us in dullness when we felt sad, and extolling our joy, showing off Ma's balloons and crepe paper when we were festive. Dad purchased the place sometime between Dorothea and Jackie from a florist named Kennedy—no relationship to *The Kennedys*. It was hard imagining any other family living there, though. A parlor behind French glass doors we used only at Christmastime. A knotty pine paneled kitchen. A closet-sized pantry containing a countertop and cabinet below it. A secret safe in an office wall. After eventually leaving that antique, feeling so truly at home again would take a long time. In adulthood, another vintage house and I would find each other. That other dwelling, busy protecting an immigrant family in a historic mill community, hid in my future as obscurely as my husband-to-be.

This reel of my memory continued with me galloping behind Michael. His shabby teddy tagged along under his arm like a silent little brother. Tucked in a square landing at the bottom of our bedroom stairs, Michael and I smashed plastic soldiers against each other. Sitting cross-legged in this cubby before neat stacks of cards, we declared "War" and "Go-Fish."

Another day, my big brother Andy, then about twenty-four and already married, sat at the table beside Ma looking at pictures. His plump belly jiggled under his green work uniform as he laughed with her at those images. Skipping up to him, I halted at his legs, stuck out my tongue—and flew away giggling.

"Hey, you little ... You're gonna get a lick'n." Our big brothers always threatened to beat us, but never did. His shouting faded as I skedaddled down the hallway to the safety of our playroom, an unfinished space at the front of the house, holding an obstacle course of toys.

In her pantry, Ma peered through pointy cat-eyeglasses, studying cookbooks as a sentry in his guardhouse examines logbooks. I pranced up to her.

"Ma, can we look in the glass?" I asked.

My mother reached up into a cabinet, removed a juice glass holding tissue paper tucked inside. She stooped to my level, picked at the stiff paper. I watched. Ma revealed a small sparkly white stone.

"What's that, Ma?" I asked, even though I'd heard the story maybe a dozen times before.

"It's a diamond," she said. "I found it under the seat of a junk car behind Dad's garage. Someday, I'm having a ring made for you with this stone."

"Can I hold it, Ma?" I asked.

"No, we must keep it here, so we don't lose it," she said.

She tucked the gem back into its cocoon and hid the glass behind the cabinet framework.

In another scene from a few years earlier in my childhood, Ma came home holding a baby. I felt bewildered.

"This is your new brother, Donnie," Ma said.

"Where did *he* come from?" I asked.

"From there," she said, pointing to the Jesus figurine on that shelf above the TV.

Staring at the small statue, I wondered how that baby could come out of it.

"Donnie is very special," Ma said.

"He doesn't look special to me," I said.

Ma laughed, lifted her apron, wiped a tear, hugged me.

My scene cuts to a tray with bumpy red plaid towels on our windowsill—rolls rising for dinner. On Wednesdays seven of us sat at our kitchen table eating spaghetti and meatballs. Ma trotted from counter to table, fridge to table, oven to table, grabbing last-minute *thises* and *thats* for our meal. Dorothea zoomed spoonfuls of food toward Donnie who sat in his highchair.

"Vrooom, vrooooom," my sister said. "Open your mouth wide. Here it comes."

Donnie chuckled, opened his mouth. She slid in orange mush— mashed potatoes and carrots. On Fridays we ate baked haddock. Saturdays, we slurped down bowls of hot dog stew in our living room, watching *Wide World of Sports* on black and white TV.

In the morning, Ma stood on our red-white-red kitchen floor at the stove, making our favorite breakfast, something she called Popeye eggs. She left her Winchester to smolder on the edge of an ashtray while pulling a slice of Wonder Bread from a bag. Using a butter knife, she cut a half-dollar hole in its center. Smeared both sides with butter and fried one side until golden brown. She flipped it over, cracked and dropped an egg into that hole while the other side browned. She lifted her cigarette to her lips, drew a long drag, and watched her creation cook, while lifting her chin, exhaling stratus clouds up to our kitchen ceiling. Ma tapped an ash off into the ashtray. With a spatula in her other hand, she flipped the bread and its egg face-down to get the white cooked just right. Sundays, Michael and I ate our traditional holy day breakfast of tenderloin steak and gravy over our beloved buttered Wonder Bread.

"Is it good, Elizabeth?" Ma asked, looking at an empty chair where my imaginary friend sat.

"Elizabeth says she likes it, Ma," I said.

I served as Elizabeth's translator, except when I misbehaved. Then Ma set Elizabeth against me by mentioning how nicely Elizabeth behaved and asking why I couldn't act more like her. This made me angry at a friend who didn't exist—and I'd wait a day or so before bringing Elizabeth back into our world.

"Two-four-seven to Nine-one-three," a female dispatcher blasted to a patrolman. *Static.* "Can you head over to Gorham Street? Woman says her son's threatening to hit his father with an axe."

I went upstairs to our dark bathroom, not to pee, but to play. I stood on tiptoes at the white soapstone sink holding a dollie a few feet from our clawfoot tub. Grasping the doll by the legs with one hand, I lathered her hair using bar soap. With the other, I rinsed her head under our faucet. Her hair became a matted rag, and I wondered how it would ever become smooth and shiny again. There laid a pile of naked dollies on the floor beside me. Picking up a black-haired one next, I did the same. Then I washed the hair of another doll in my pile. So it went until bored of washing dollie hair, I noticed Dad's retractable razor cartridge. Lifted and held it. Examined it, pressing its parts this way and that. A thin slice of metal slid out and fell into our wet sink. It stuck there. I peeled it off.

The sharp blade stung my flesh, inflaming my finger, triggering, "Maaaaaaaa."

Bright red droplets trickled into the sink.

The back steps creaked as Ma scolded me while climbing up, "How many times do I have to tell you …" She reached our bathroom door. "… not to touch," synchronizing the highest pitch of her rant, with the whack on my bottom.

I cried. Ma fished a bandage from a tin in our medicine cabinet, wrapped my finger, then hugged me into her apron.

"What a mess," she said. "Look at your dollies and look at you! You look like nobody owns you!"

Leaving the mess to her, I bolted downstairs, across our kitchen, and out the door. I passed Virgin Mary watching over our little yard. These statues were popular back then. Made of plaster, the Holy Mother stood in blue robes within a scalloped cement frame, like a *Mary on the Half-Shell*. Ma's brother, Uncle Bud, painted her face white, eyes blue, and hair brown. Ours rose three-feet tall, counting a stone pedestal. I scuttled under the canopy of Michael's weeping willow towering over her.

Ma always said they planted that willow when Michael was born and "look how tall it is already."

This made me jealous. I didn't have a special tree. Two crabapple trees, one on each side of a walkway, greeted visitors from our driveway—a dirt driveway that horseshoed up, around our house, and back down to the road. At the top, tall flowers and ground covers brimmed over the white rock border of Ma's garden.

I dashed around a corner to a nook under our house, just outside an obsolete entryway where a rusty metal door led into our cellar. Through its dusty window, I peered into our dark basement at pairs of skates, dry cleaning clothes, boxes, and broken furniture. Constructed of two stone walls opposite each other, the alcove hid under our house's framing, shielding it from heat and rain. Here, the old house embraced me. It observed and forgave me.

A few minutes later, I scampered back inside. Ma sat on her tattered green leather chair with casters. She wheeled herself between a long desk where she managed Dad's car shop billing and her black Singer sewing machine, where she hemmed and mended our clothes. Michael and I played at her feet.

Ma got up, removed a landscape painting from the wall, and turned a dial on a metal box a smidgen one way, a smidgen the other way. My mother opened that safe door and placed envelopes inside. She closed the metal door, turned the dial back and forth, and replaced the picture over it.

On weekdays, Ma dressed me in a plaid dress adorned by a lacy collar and clipped a bow into my curly permed hair. She waved goodbye as I climbed onto a yellow school bus headed for South Row Elementary School. I found my seat in Mrs. Gray's second-grade classroom. Mrs. Gray stood tall and slender and kept her brown hair short with bangs. She wore pointy glasses like Ma's, but dark brown ones without the sparkles. Mrs. Gray danced a little jig on the way to her seat each morning. She spent late afternoons reading aloud. In one story, a little girl refuses to bathe. Her parents wait until she falls asleep. Then they plant radish seeds into the dirt on top of her skin. Next morning when the girl awakens, radishes sprout from her body. She freaks out and demands a bath and never refuses bathing again. Years later, I remembered Betty MacDonald's *Mrs. Piggle-Wiggle* story well enough to hunt it down and read it to my own children.

Yet as hard as I try, I can't dredge up from memory or public records why on Thursday, March 21, 1968, Michael and I stayed home from school. Some details of that day remain clear as glass, others, as murky as chocolate pudding. A few of the day's events are gone, inaccessible. On that Thursday morning, I slunk into the kitchen and found Ma in her guardhouse reading her cookbooks.

Standing before her, I whimpered. Felt afraid.

"Ma, I'm sorry, but I peed my bed again," I said.

"I'm sick and tired of this," Ma yelled and sighed and slammed her cookbook shut.

I followed Ma's thick ankles and oxfords stomping up the stairs. She ripped the sheets off my bed. Ranted about this. Ranted about that. Shoved in corners of clean sheets. Ma rough handled me into dry clothes. I followed her chubby arms full of my sodden bed linens and pajamas down the stairs.

"Go to your room," she screamed.

In this frame, I see myself lie on top of that clean bed and fall asleep. While I sank into my covers, Ma stepped into the basement. Meantime, a group of friends met Michael down the street. In the basement, Ma looped an end of electrical cord. Those neighborhood boys invited Michael to skate on a pond. Ma placed a chair under a wooden rafter. Michael ran home for his skates. Ma stood and steadied herself on the chair. She tied the cord over the cross beam above. She tugged it, testing its strength. Tired, Michael began walking. He had a few blocks to go. Ma placed her head into the loop. Slightly tightened the device. Stepped off the chair.

A short while later, Michael got home, raced down our basement steps. Scanned the dark room for his skates. Instead, my brother spotted our mother's feet and legs suspended. Then he noticed the hem of her dress. He looked up. Ma's head rested limp on her shoulder. Michael ran back upstairs, out the door, across a field to Dad's car repair shop. Michael returned with Andy. Crying, Andy in his green, grease-soiled uniform grabbed and up righted the chair, stepped on it, managed taking Ma down. Sitting on that chair in our dingy basement amid dusty boxes and suits and fancy dresses draped in dry cleaner's plastic, Andy cradled Ma in his lap and sobbed.

Dad in his own grease-soiled uniform and Uncle Johnny in his black dress pants and white shirt rushed to the basement.

"Oh my God," Dad cried. And cried.

An ambulance arrived. Paramedics carried a stretcher into the basement. They placed Ma on it, hoisted it upstairs, wheeled her up into the ambulance, secured doors, and drove her away.

I remained asleep on my bed, two floors above where Uncle Johnny found me a short while later.

Chapter 2

One of the last things Ma said to me was, "I'm sick and tired of this." *This.* That meant me. She was sick and tired of me. As a mother myself now, I consider all the ways over the years my kids made me "sick and tired of 'this.'"

At about six, my son Geoff one morning spilled a puddle of maple syrup on the floor, danced in it in bare feet, and ran down a hallway, requiring me to wash the feet and floor on the spot. At about eight, he dismantled an electric pencil sharpener, cut the cord off it, and spliced its wires into those of a small electric radio. He then plugged his Frankenstein-ified appliance into a wall socket and shut down electricity to our entire house.

As a baby until almost two, my son Greg screamed nonstop in his car seat, quelling weekend getaways and nonessential car trips. Couldn't sit in a grocery cart either. I'd be in produce one minute, then chasing him down frozen foods the next. At two, he went into all-out temper tantrums demanding ice cream for breakfast nearly every morning. At three, he bit a little girl's cheek at the Gale Library in Newton, New Hampshire, creating an acute purple welt on her face. If the daggers shooting from her mother's eyes were real, he and I would both be maimed for life. At five and eight, my boys swung plastic swords in the house, once striking a ceiling light fixture, sending it smashing down onto Geoff's head and sending us rushing to the emergency room for sutures. And to the ER we rushed after Greg, at about three, fell off a cliff at Purgatory Chasm, a popular hiking spot in Sutton, Massachusetts. During childhood, they threw up *and peed* in their beds, broke windows and lanterns, smashed fists, and slung mud at each other, friends, and enemies. Reframed by my own experiences as a mom, I no longer believe I sent my mother to her grave over bed-wetting.

That realization would take decades to arrive. Until then, Ma's departure clung onto my heart like a sock. A sock soaked in kerosene, a little more each year, preparing for the magnificent bonfire we'd ignite as my pain readied itself for revelation. When the remaining white-hot embers burnt out, I'd finally awake back in what felt like my own bed, in my own home—nearly half a century away.

A few days after Ma died, I got back on the bus for South Row, my elementary school in Chelmsford. On the way to my second-grade classroom, a classmate stopped me in the hallway and offered some Oreos in a plastic sandwich bag.

"No thanks," I said.

He regarded me, pursed his lips, and disappeared. Less familiar children approached, said they were sorry. A teacher or other grownup must have told them about Ma. That they should be nice to me. That they should say "I'm sorry" when they see me back at school.

Mrs. Gray greeted me at our classroom door, took my hand as she scolded some boys about running inside. She led me back out into the hallway and knelt at my level. A racket of children's laughter and chaos echoing in hallways melted away as she began speaking.

"These things sometimes happen," she said. I waited for her to continue, but that was it. I followed her back into the classroom. Took my seat.

At home, we talked about Ma only when necessary, like as Dorothea explained mixing and mashing boiled potatoes and carrots and butter for us kids.

"That's how Ma always did it," she said.

As a child, I discussed Ma during private deals with God. With my eighth birthday approaching, I prayed, "God, can I have a new bicycle because I lost Ma?"

My birthday came, I got the bike, thanked Him, and kept score. He still owed me. Another day, I prayed, "God, can you help me go for ice cream today because I lost Ma?" I also got chances to mention Ma when people didn't know what happened. A new teacher might say, "Bring that paper home for your mother to sign."

"My mother died," I'd say.

I liked opportunities to say it.

"Oh, I'm so sorry," my teacher might say. It felt comforting when people expressed sympathy, like a small soothing hug.

Dorothea and Bob got married as they planned in August 1968. Dad had Ma's parlor and French doors torn out. Converted the space into a bedroom for the newlyweds. Carpenters installed an additional bathroom where Ma's billing desk and sewing machine had been. They turned our front playroom into a living room for Dorothea and Bob. Renovations covered the grate in the floor and the safe in the wall.

Dorothea quit her secretarial job and sacrificed her freedom to stay home and take care of Michael, Donnie, and me. Creativity became her escape. She painted and baked ceramic pottery. Transformed fabric and yarn into Raggedy Ann dolls. Needled satin embroidery floss into cloth, creating fancy pillowcases and napkins.

Whatever life Dorothea dreamed of having before Ma died would never be. As a young wife, she cooked and cleaned for our family of eight, which included her new husband. Dad came home from work most nights, had dinner with us. Then he went upstairs and bounced down wearing a clean dress shirt and slacks. He paused to laugh with us as Donnie sat on the floor putting on and taking off oversized hats and peering up at their brims. Then Dad disappeared for the night, leaving a waft of Old Spice in his wake.

I figured out by then why Ma considered Donnie "special." Donnie has Down syndrome. No one took me aside and explained Donnie's disability to me. It just became apparent. His small eyes are shaped like almonds and slant upwards at the outermost corners. As a child, he seemed so flexible at times as to have soft bones. His big toe juts out, leaving a large gap between it and his other toes. He calls this toe his *onka*. He moans a happy moan and sometimes looks sideways at one hand. He once yanked my hair so hard I thought it would come out. Another time, he bit my chest until it bled. He disregarded most social norms. Openly displayed love and rage to optimal potentials. At school, only "mentally retarded" kids, as they were called back then, acted this way.

Named after the physician who first characterized the condition, Down syndrome occurs in babies who develop an extra full or partial copy of chromosome 21 in all or some of their cells. It can originate from mothers or fathers at conception. It's not believed to be caused by environmental factors or either parent's lifestyle choices or behaviors. Advanced maternal age can be a factor, but today, eighty percent of kids with Down syndrome are born to moms under thirty-five years of age.

Whatever its origin, this microscopic detail prevented Donnie's normal physical and cognitive development. In Donnie's case, he would never read, drive, drink with his buddies, take a girl to the dance, get laid, marry, have children and a great job, or shave his own beard.[1] He'd also never miss doing any of these things. It was Dorothea and Bob who sacrificed.

Besides creativity, Dorothea's only relief from caring for us three kids came during her weekend date nights with Bob. On Sunday mornings, Dorothea got us dressed and to church. Dad and Bob stayed home.

In the car, I asked, "Why don't Dad and Bob come with us, Dor?"

"Because they are heathens," she replied.

I didn't know what heathens were. I sensed it meant they hated God or were against attending church. Ma never took us to church, and she wasn't a heathen. She said Donnie came from baby Jesus. She had a Virgin Mary in the yard.

On the way home, we stopped at Dunkin' Donuts. Dorothea let us choose our favorite treats. Donnie and I always got marshmallow donuts—cake pockets with soft, sugary cream inside, and powdered sugar outside. Michael got a cruller, a long crispy-crusted donut with

---

[1] As a side note, many people with Down syndrome experience mild to moderate cognitive delays. Many live happy, long, and nearly independent lives due to medical, societal, and educational advances. People with Down syndrome may have some of the physical traits associated with the condition or none at all.

jelly inside and granulated sugar outside. Dorothea got chocolate and other donuts, making a dozen box. We ate them when we got home instead of our usual tenderloin on Wonder Bread.

"Should I call you Ma?" I asked Dorothea.

"No, I'm your sister," she snapped back.

We went through this refrain many times over the years.

One evening, Dorothea and Bob went out while we stayed home under the watch of our babysitter. They later came home and discovered one of Dorothea's creations—a ceramic pumpkin—broken. It seemed plausible only Michael, Donnie, or I could have done it. Next morning we kids went on trial.

"Did you break the pumpkin?" she asked, looking at Michael.

"No," he said.

Still fuming, she turned to me, asked, "Did you break the pumpkin, Mary Gayle? You better tell me the truth."

"Nooooo," I said.

"Donnie, did you break the pumpkin?" she asked, looking at Donnie.

"No," he said, chuckling. He thought we were playing a game.

"Someone's lying," she said.

What happened next remained etched in our memories so well that later in life at my son, Geoffrey's, eighth birthday party, while watching him open gifts, Michael leaned into my ear and whispered, "Did you break the pumpkin?"

However, let's remember these were the actions of a loving sister, but also a young twenty-something-year-old saddled with a burden greater than anything someone that age should endure.

She grabbed one of Michael's hands, switched on an electric stovetop burner to low, as I watched, terrified. She held his hand over the coil and repeated herself.

"Did you break the pumpkin?" she said.

"No," he cried.

She let go of his hand. He ran off. She grabbed my arm.

"No," I shrieked, trying to yank my arm away. She managed pulling me over to the stove. She held my hand over the burner, against my resistance.

"Did you break the pumpkin?" she asked.

"No," I cried, tears pouring down my face.

She let me go, shut off the burner.

"God'll punish whoever did it," she said, and began clearing off the table.

As children after finishing breakfast, Michael and I liked racing down the hall to play, but after Ma died, he wasn't home much. After school, he hung out with friends or did odd jobs for Dad at his garage.

"God, can we do something special this week because I lost Ma?" I prayed.

Dorothea and Bob took us fishing, to country fairs, amusement parks, and out for dinners. One day about a year following Ma's death, Dorothea cleaned the cabinet above our kitchen sink. I noticed her lifting that juice glass holding tissue paper.

"That's mine," I said.

"What is it?" she said, tugging at the tissue.

"Be careful. My diamond is in there," I said.

She brought it down to my level, like Ma did, and picked at the tissue, revealing the small stone.

"Ma found it and she was gonna have a ring made for me with it," I said.

"Oh, I'll save it for you, okay?" she said.

"Okay," I said.

Dorothea folded the tissue back around the stone, returned it to its juice glass, hid the glass back in our cupboard.

We were settling in without Ma.

All the while, Jackie made chaos rain down on us. One evening, Dorothea was cooking dinner. I was coloring at our kitchen table.

"Nine-one-three to Two-four-seven," a patrolman shouted over Dad's police scanner. "Send an ambulance to Route 495 north bound lane ..."

The officer gave directions for the ambulance, somewhere along that highway in Chelmsford. "Got a guy here stabbed with an ice pick. He's in stable condition but must be checked out. No suspect at the scene."

"Two-four-seven to Nine-one-three, ambulance on the way. Got a name?"

"John J. Ferreira."

I glanced at the radio. Dorothea rushed over to it, turned it up. Did this because Jackie's real name was John. *He was* John J. Ferreira.

"F as in Frank. E as in elephant. R as in Robert …" That night, a police officer knocked on the door. Dorothea stepped outside to speak with him. Later from my bed I heard Dad yelling and Jackie crying.

"What the hell is wrong wit you, Jackie?" Dad said.

I got out of bed and stood in our upstairs hallway, yearning for my floor grate.

"I don't know, Dad," Jackie said. He sniffled, gasped for breaths between high pitched cries and whimpers, then said, "I'm sorry."

"Stop actin' like a goddamned baby, Jackie," Dad said. "It's time to grow up and act like a man. Snap out of it!"

I didn't understand Dad's anger toward Jackie since he was the one attacked by some bad guy wielding an ice pick. Many years later, I learned Jackie inflicted those wounds on himself, hoping for drugs alongside sutures. I still felt sorry for him because there wasn't a difference. The bad guy brandishing the ice pick was real. He lived inside Jackie's head.

There were better days, though, too. On a Saturday during springtime 1969, Dad rolled up our driveway in a brand-new motor home—a wide bus containing fewer windows. It had two beige lightning bolts pinstriped along its outside. Dorothea, Bob, Michael, Donnie, and I all rushed outside.

"Dad, did you buy it?" I asked.

"Yep," he said, standing beside it like a proud chauffeur. "Go in and see."

Inside, this house on wheels had a compact kitchen and beds and a bathroom. Michael ran down the narrow aisle to the back and belly flopped onto a bed.

"I love it, Dad," I said, as I pulled open cabinets, doors, drawers. Dorothea, Bob, and Donnie took seats at a compact kitchen table.

"It's like taking all your housework with you on vacation," Dorothea said, sighing.

Donnie explored his hand cross-eyed and twitched—like he always does in excitement—and let out his happy groan, "Ooouuuuuuu."

Michael ran back down the narrow aisle, hopped into the driver's seat, twisted the steering wheel back and forth, pretending to drive. I opened a thin door and peered into a tiny bathroom, amazed at its miniature apparatus.

Occasionally, Dad, Dorothea, Bob, Michael, Donnie, and I piled in. Dad and Bob took turns driving us to mountains in New Hampshire or Vermont. Other times Dad loaded his motor home up with me, Michael, Donnie, and all the neighborhood kids, who were our cousins, for trips to Kimball Farms ice cream stand. Perhaps there were eight or ten of us—boys, girls, assorted ages, heights, widths.

As the motor home slowed to stop, we lined up inside to exit. Kimball's operated in a long brown barn with six small sliding screened windows. We'd queue up again at a window and wait in a line dozens of people deep.

Inside Kimball's, a hive of teenagers wearing chocolate-smudged white aprons over tees and dungaree fringed shorts rushed this way and that—scoops in one hand, cones in the other. Torsos leaned into ice chests, one foot off the ground behind them. Constant bug zapping by the neon taser overhead. Still plenty of mosquitoes to swat off my sweaty arms and legs while considering choices.

"Get whateva ya want," Dad said to his tribe.

I made a decision based on a waft of steaming chocolate from a stranger's hot fudge sundae as he rushed past me toward the gold Pontiac where his chubby wife waited on the passenger's side.

"Did you remember napkins?" she called as he got closer.

Women waiting in line bounced inpatient toddlers on a hip. Kids playing tag zigzagged between patrons in line while their parents scolded them to "stop running around."

"Hi," I said, waving at a boy from school who passed by. His eyes darted at and past me. He said nothing, because he didn't want his big brother knowing he talked to the fat girl at school. Any sympathy I got from him after Ma died had worn off by then.

Finally, it was our turn.

"Get whateva ya want," Dad repeated.

We ordered sundaes and banana splits and root beer floats and ice cream cones. Michael got "The Kitchen Sink," a meal-sized cardboard boat jam-packed with vanilla, chocolate, and strawberry ice cream, bananas, melted marshmallow, hot fudge, whipped cream, nuts, and a cherry. Dad ordered his usual, a strawberry soda—always a strawberry soda. I got a hot fudge sundae. Even a small size held about a pint of ice cream, a cup of hot fudge, enough whipped cream to fill a beer mug.

"Uncle Tony, I have my own money," some of the cousins said, digging crumpled dollars from their pockets.

"Put ya money away," Dad scorned as he fetched a thick wad of cash from his pocket and paid for the whole lot.

We marched away from the mayhem, back to the motorhome parked across the street, as crickets blew their broken whistles.

If I visited Dad's garage as a kid, I had better have something productive to do.

"This is no place for a girl," he'd often say, which was fine with me.

I took no interest whatsoever in cars, tools, and auto supplies, except for one item: car wax. I loved how you could smear the vanilla muck on a dull fender and wipe it away, leaving the car sparkling like a crystal lake on a sunny day. That's why I often parked my bike behind Dad's garage—out of the sight—and dug out a cloth from his clean rag bag and grabbed a fat tin of his car wax to shine it up. The year must have been about 1970. Summertime. Done rinsing the bike down with Dad's hose and drying it off, I dipped a rag into the hard, buttery stuff and slathered it over my handlebars. I polished them to a gloss, then inspected the black left behind on the rag.

Dad strolled over, drying his hands with a paper towel, and said, "There's someone I'd like ya ta meet."

Chapter 3

I followed Dad past a workbench heaping with wrenches, chisels, pliers, an assortment of hammers. We walked under a car on a lift, through the big bay door to a maroon station wagon parked out front. A lady wearing short brown hair, paper white skin, and bright red lipstick smiled at us from the driver's side.

"This is Eleana," Dad said.

"Hi, you must be Mary Gayle," Eleanor said. "Your father has told me a lot about you."

By the end of our conversation, I agreed to a shopping trip with her.

Eleanor was about thirty-eight. Dad was about fifty. I walked across the field to our home. Large spikey plants cracked through the asphalt walkway around the house. In our kitchen, Donnie, about six by then and obsessed over baseball, stepped up to his imaginary home plate. In his imagination, he didn't just *imitate* Carl Yastrzemski; he *was* Carl Yastrzemski. He tapped his plastic bat on the floor a few times, took several practice swings, swaying from side to side. Holding his bat high, making it twitch back and forth, like the pro, he stood poised and ready. Dorothea pitched a plastic whiffle ball from a few feet away. Donnie slammed it, sending the ball soaring. He ran his imaginary bases, tapping his foot on each one along the way, then threw up his hands in victory as he reached home plate. We laughed. I forgot about Dad and Eleanor and took over pitching while Dorothea got dinner ready.

A few days later, Dad said Eleanor would take me shopping on Saturday morning.

"Eleanor is taking me shopping on Saturday," I said to Dorothea.

"Yeah, well, she's not your mother. Just remember that," Dorothea said.

That Saturday morning, Eleanor drove up the driveway. I ran out and hopped into the car. Driving into Boston, she inquired about Dad and our family. What Ma was like and how we were getting along since she died. I told her Ma was the most beautiful woman I ever saw. I shared other details about what had been happening since Ma died as best as I could, likely not mentioning the broken pumpkin.

At Filene's Basement we shopped for girls' dresses. She asked if I liked long granny dresses, the calico print ones with puffy sleeves. Other girls at school wore them. I didn't know how I'd ever get one. Ma always ordered our clothes from *Sears* catalog. Eleanor helped me choose one and try it on. Then she bought it for me. We had lunch at a nearby café where I continued updating her on details of our family and relatives. She dropped me off after dinnertime. Inside, Dorothea washed a pile of dirty dishes.

"Did you have a nice time with Mumsy?" she said.

"Why are you calling her that?" I asked.

"Because you act like she's your mother," she said.

"No I don't," I said.

Michael joined the taunt, "Yeah how was your day with Mumsy?" he said.

"Stop saying that," I said.

Eleanor came often. She took me to her house across town and introduced me to her three sons Jeffrey, who was about eight; David, about twelve; and Randy, about fifteen. Sometimes she took me and Jeff to the Garrison House, our town's oldest home. She picked a leaf of oregano from the herb garden there and demonstrated rubbing it between her thumb and forefinger, then smelling its fragrance. I rubbed and sniffed thyme and mint, then rosemary and tarragon. Sometimes we baked cookies and other goodies at her house. She taught me how to sift flour and never pack it into measuring cups.

"But you do want to pack brown sugar," she said as she demonstrated pushing the soft, moist sugar into a measuring cup using a spoon, and a butter knife to level it off. "I make everything from scratch. Why buy cake mix when it tastes so much better? And it's so easy."

Jeff and I went outside to see his pony, Flash, and his beagle, Gus. Other times, Dad came, and we ate dinner with Eleanor and her sons. Sometimes, Michael joined us. They didn't usually invite Donnie.

At Eleanor's sink one day, I washed dishes. Eleanor dried them.

"I always wanted a daughter," she said, passing a pan back to me. "Oops, this one needs more scrubbing," she said.

She mentioned you could tell if a pan was clean by feeling its insides.

"If it's smooth, you know it's clean, but if it's bumpy, it needs more scrubbing," she said.

"I help my sista do dishes sometimes," I lied.

"It's not sista," she corrected my Boston accent. "It's sisTER."

"SisTER," I repeated, imitating her accentuation of "TER."

She explained how as a young girl, she had polio. Nurses forced her to sit in a tub of "hot, hot water, as hot as I could stand it." She said during World War II, some officials collected her family's sterling silver and melted it for "war efforts." She kept a little book of "poeeems" in her apron pocket and read them aloud. She said she worked for the telephone company as an operator. Crazy people called her up all the time.

Back then everyone sought an operator's help on a daily basis. Sometimes several times a day. At a time without smartphones to store contact information and no internet to look up numbers, you called Directory Assistance at no extra charge. If you experienced trouble getting through or felt too lazy to dial or needed an ambulance or the police pronto, you could just dial zero and an operator would connect you.

"Sometimes they're just looking for a laugh," she said. "'You and me are getting engaged, right?' they'll say," she explained. "I'll say, 'Yeah right.' Then the guy will go 'Oh so that's how you treat a man who just gave you a ring,'" she laughs. "They must have nothing better to do."

Back home later, Dorothea, Michael, and when around, Jackie teased me about my day with "Mumsy," and I began to sense a distancing between us.

Dad packed the camper and took me, Michael, Donnie, Eleanor, and her youngest son, Jeffrey, to Barnard, Vermont. Eleanor's two other sons preferred and were old enough to stay home alone. We traveled to see my godparents, Uncle Sonny, Ma's brother and his wife, Auntie Jeannie. Uncle Sonny wore dress slacks and shirts during weekdays, not work clothes like Dad. Uncle Sonny's face missed his dark-rimmed glasses when he removed them. He almost always smiled and as wide as the cartoon character, Yogi Bear.

A petite woman, Auntie Jeannie coddled me in her sympathetic voice. It's not what she said, but how she said it, like a kind person might talk to a puppy who needs a good home. Uncle Sonny and Auntie Jeannie had three daughters, all older than me—in high school and college. When we arrived, they seemed thrilled to see and escort us into their house, even though we showed up unannounced. We sat around their table, as Dad shared jokes and stories. In his stories, he was the foolish protagonist taking mishaps in stride, learning from them.

"When Route 495 first went in, we'd get a lot of nuts coming 'round the garage."

Auntie Jeannie glanced at me and smiled, scrunching up her nose, knowing we were in for a treat with one of Dad's tales.

"One day a guy came by and said, 'You wanna buy a pair a shoes?'
'What size?'
He said, 'All sizes, two dollas a pair.'
The guy opened his trunk, and it was fulla boxes a shoes. Nice. Black. Men's patent leatha shoes."

Dad ran a hand along the smooth exterior of an imaginary shoe he held in his other hand and regarded each of us. Our eyes stayed glued on him. No one made a peep.

"I said, 'How much for the whole lot?'
'A dolla a pair.'
I told him, 'I'll take the whole trunk full.'
The guy helped me set 'em up in the station near the window. Next day, the oil man, John Quinn, stopped by.
I said, 'Hey John, need a pair a shoes?'
'How much?'
'Two dollas a pair.'"

Everyone cracked up.

"*So he bought a pair.*

Later that day, John came back and said, 'Tony, ya know those shoes I bought from you?'

'Yeah, what about 'em?'

'They're both for left feet.'

'Oh, well come on over, and we'll switch one with anotha pair.'

We went through every single goddamned box and ya know something? They were all left feet."

Everyone laughed, including Dad, at his own story. Eleanor's laugh came with a roll of her eyes.

As we left, I overheard Auntie Jeannie mention to Dad she was happy he "found someone."

Not long afterwards, Dad told me I wouldn't be seeing Eleanor anymore. He said it just didn't work. He handed me a note inside a pink smiley face envelope secured by a sealing wax stamp. Eleanor wrote she was sorry we couldn't see each other anymore, but she was glad to get to know me. It was more puzzling than sad. What was the problem?

About a week later, though, Eleanor returned. She talked with Dad at his garage. Then shopping and dinner invitations and camping trips and visits to relatives continued. We never discussed the letter inside the pink smiley face envelope.

Dorothea and Bob soon announced they were moving out. That they'd come and check on us often, though. Around 1971, they found an apartment in Danvers, Massachusetts, about thirty-five minutes south of Chelmsford. I turned eleven by then. Dad dubbed me the lady of the house.

A bus came for Donnie weekday mornings. I watched him after school and on weekends. This ended up a short-term arrangement.

One Saturday, I baked a cake for Dad because it was his birthday. Dad was working. I didn't know where Michael and Jackie were. While I had never baked a three-tier cake, I had it figured out. After all, I had watched Ma cook for years, and Eleanor taught me about baking from scratch. I greased and floured pans, placed them on the table. Sifted and measured flour, dumped it in a bowl. Measured baking powder, dumped it in.

Across the room, Donnie, sitting on the floor, began crying.

"Wait, Donnie. I am busy," I said.

He continued crying. In went cocoa powder and the remaining dry ingredients. I put that bowl aside. Donnie cried louder.

"Wait, Donnie," I said.

I took another bowl. Measured butter, dumped it in. Measured sugar, dumped it in the bowl, along with eggs and vanilla and the remaining wet stuff. Grabbing a hand-held electric mixer, I sank the beaters into the dry ingredients, turned it on. A cloud of dark powder billowed up, leaving its brown dust on the countertop and floor.

I mixed wet ingredients and poured the dry stuff into it. I turned the mixer back on. Donnie cried louder. I ignored him. Dorothea walked in.

"What are you doing?" she said.

"I'm makin' a cake for Dad's birthday," I said.

She scanned the countertop, the bowls, the flour dust. She looked at Donnie, still wailing. She put her hand on her cheek and began crying, too. She picked up Donnie and hugged him. She took him into the bathroom, then came back.

"I'm taking Donnie," she said.

"Okay," I said.

As she carried him out, I continued on my project, relieved they both left. I didn't know then this was a sign of things to come. That Dorothea would sacrifice her freedom to protect Donnie, and I'd get to keep making and cleaning up my own messes.

Jackie popped in and out of our lives. Sometimes clean. Sometimes not. During a clean spell, he took Michael and me to Zyla's auction. Inside a cold warehouse containing hundreds of rows and rows of white folding chairs, Zyla's auctioned off everything from wrapping paper to wheelbarrows on the cheap. Among many items for sale that night, came mixed-breed puppies or mutts as they were called back then.

"Aww," the audience cooed.

"Oh," I said. "Can I have one?"

"Me, too," Michael said.

Jackie's hand shot up. He won the bid, each pup costing two dollars. The auctioneer handed us the two puppies and boxes layered in wood shavings. Michael claimed the brown dog with upright ears. I loved my white one with black spots and floppy ears. We cuddled them the whole way home, arguing over whose dog was better while blurting out possible names. I named mine Rinney, after a garage dog Dad had years ago. Jackie stopped for dog food. When we got home, Dad, sitting in his living room chair, twisted his head around, shooting a quizzical look at those boxes.

"Dad, look what Jackie got us at the auction," I said, showing him my puppy inside. Michael took his pup out and let it sniff around.

"Goddamnit, Jackie." Dad hollered. "What the hell is wrong wit you!"

"Dad, I'll take care of mine," I said. "Can we please keep them?"

"I'll take care of mine, too, Dad," Michael said.

Jackie stood by grinning.

"I don't want any goddamned messes around here so help me God," Dad said, shaking his head and smacking his lips and sighing several times.

"You keep them goddamned things in the garage downstairs."

He looked at Jackie, "What the hell, Jackie! Do you have a screw loose?"

Next day, Eleanor brought me a book about puppy care. I read it from cover to cover that same day. My favorite chapter provided step-by-step illustrated instructions on teaching your dog tricks. Every chance I got, I walked down the creaky cellar steps, into our dark basement, past the spot where Ma died, although I still didn't know that then, on my way to the garage to feed and train Rinney. I taught him to stay, to come when called, to walk on a leash, and roll over—all with the incentive of only pats on his head and belly, not dog treats. In one of my few diary entries. I wrote about him in my little girl prose, typos, and lollypop dots on my *i's* and all.

> When 'your' sad, who do you go to? To your Dad or to your mother? To an older sister or brother? Do you just go and sit around worrying? Do you take a walk or go and look at the stars at night?
>
> I 'now' it's very dumb and kind of crazy, but I go to my dog. He's a little guy I can always depend on. I'm

sure he can keep a secret. He seems to listen to me, even though I know he's not. He's a little mongrel with bloodshot eyes, whose name is Rinney. He's actually a treat for the family, especially me. After all he belongs to me with all his little tricks. He brings fun to my family. Whenever I get mad at him, he 'crowches' way down and puts his head between his legs. He does this so I'll feel bad for him and pat him and shake hands and be friends and it works and that is only one of his little tricks.

When Rinney was full grown, I let him loose outside and he roamed the neighborhood as he pleased, and he always came back home.

Rusty bikes that Michael and I neglected and a few junk cars Dad and Jackie had accumulated began filling up our yard. Ma's crabapple trees got chopped down because Dor said its miniature apples spotted the walkway. Someone also chopped down Michael's big willow tree because it also made too much work in fall. Seeing it gone disappointed me, even though I felt jealous about it as a smaller child. We were supposed to see how tall the tree got as Michael grew up. Ma's garden in the middle of the driveway had more weeds than flowers. Paint on Virgin Mary's face and robes started peeling. A corner of her half shell had chipped off.

Inside, our dryer sat in the middle of our kitchen floor on the fritz for weeks. Dad meant to fix it. Week-old newspapers cluttered the kitchen table. Every Monday night, Dad and I strolled up and down aisles at Star Market, grabbing canned beans and soup, TV dinners, milk, and cereal, and all the rest. Most nights for supper, Dad ordered dinner from George's, a local deli where he picked up food at lunchtime for his garage employees. We used newspapers as placemats.

At dinnertime, a customer came to see Dad. I invited him in. He stood there, talking to Dad who sat at the table before his dinner plate atop newspapers dated probably the month before. As Dad spoke, he alternated glances at the man with looks at that newspaper, of which Dad held a corner—as if he were reading something real important in that outdated paper. That's how I knew the mess embarrassed Dad. That maybe I better throw away those old papers after dinner.

Dad and Eleanor arranged for me to spend a week during late summer 1972 in Vermont with Uncle Sonny and Auntie Jeannie, who seemed glad to have me there. Their porch wrapped around the house front. Their high living room ceiling reached up to a loft with bannisters and a railing. The size of their kitchen exceeded anything I'd ever seen. Floors were clean. Countertops uncluttered. No stacks of newspapers on tables or anywhere else. Everything tidy and spacious. Surrounded by acres and acres of land, they had only one neighbor opposite their home. My cousin, Donna, about fourteen and the youngest of their three daughters, invited me to tag alongside her for the week—to swim in ponds, pick blueberries, and cheer on Mark Spitz as he won seven Olympic gold medals during that summer's swimming competitions.

Auntie Jeannie kept an abundant backyard vegetable garden and rows of brown eyed Susans and other flowers out front. She darted about her home like a bee on clusters of minute errands—making beds in one room, washing dishes in another, straightening a hallway closet, and packing supplies in it. She picked tomatoes and cucumbers and radishes from the garden and swept outdoor steps. While I was in the bathroom, she swept just outside its window. I pulled down my pants and droplets of blood hit the floor. I bled from "down there."

"Auntie Jeannie," I cried. "I'm bleeding."

She rushed in, explained about little girls and periods just like Dorothea and Auntie Theresa had tried doing with me the year before. Auntie Jeannie opened her hallway closet and pulled out a sanitary napkin and showed me how to use it. After we were done, she showed me where to get these supplies from the closet—and all was well again.

Uncle Sonny went to work during weekdays. As a child, I didn't know where or what he did. Whenever he saw me, he smiled his big Yogi Bear smile and asked how I was doing. On weekends, Uncle Sonny poured pancake batter into a frying pan and told me you flip them once they bubbled on one side. At their kitchen table, Auntie Jeannie scolded him about too much butter and syrup.

About a week after I'd arrived, Dad's motor home floated into the driveway, rocking back and forth like *The Beverly Hillbillies'* truck. I ran outside ahead of Uncle Sonny and Auntie Jeannie. Eleanor stepped down the three steps out of the motor home, as she always did, one step at a time, using both hands, holding tight to the railing on account of "my polio," as she always referred to the childhood disease she braved as a youngster, making her legs weaker and her adult life harder than it should have been. Her bright red lips were spread across her face in a wide smile. Dad bounced down, looking like he just hit the trifecta at the racetrack.

"We have something to tell you, Mary Gayle," she said, all giddy and excited. "We got married!"

A fleeting shock of losing something I just *in that moment* conceived of having—a little pink bridesmaid's dress and flower bouquet—flew in and out of my mind all at once. She reached out her wiggling fingers, showing off a shimmering diamond and gold wedding band. "Let me see yours, Dad," I said. His ring confirmed their union.

Why moan over missing the wedding? That they didn't tell me they were getting married? It was done and couldn't be undone and redone any other way.

"That's great," I said. "I'm happy." Because I was supposed to be happy.

Uncle Sonny and Auntie Jeannie congratulated them. Then we all went inside for a snack and a story—the story of their wedding. After leaving me with Uncle Sonny and Auntie Jeannie, Dad and Eleanor visited Amish Country in Pennsylvania and eloped. They laughed, talking about the ancient, haunted cottage where they stayed.

"We kept hearin' footsteps out on the porch," Dad said. "I thought someone was tryin' a get in."

"He stood by the door holding a broom over his head," Eleanor said.

"I was gonna whack the son-of-a-bitch as soon as he came in," Dad said.

That night, Dad, Eleanor, and I drove two and a half hours home. Dad dropped Eleanor off at her house and drove us home to our house, where we stayed that night and many nights for months to follow.

Chapter 4

We continued living apart from Eleanor while Dad hired a contractor to expand her three-bedroom home. The new space added a hallway, walk-in pantry closet, a bedroom for Dad and Eleanor, and a family room adorned with a fireplace spread across an entire wall, like the Garrison House's.

Early in their marriage, Eleanor and I were in her car talking about Donnie.

"You, know, I could never take Donnie," she said. "It's too hard for me because of my polio."

"I know," I said. "But I could help."

"What if he went with a foster family?" she asked.

"No, he's my brotha," I said.

"It's not brotha," she corrected me. "It's broTHER."

I tried again. "He's my broTHER," I repeated. "No."

"It would be a family who can care for his needs better than we can," she said.

I never knew we could lose Donnie. It seemed like they wanted to give one of us away, like families sometimes threaten to do, but never would do.

"No," I said. "Neva."

"NeVER," she corrected.

"NeVER," I repeated.

Dad soon took Michael and me to visit Donnie at a "special school," called the Fernald School. Dad said Donnie got excellent care there. A nurse led him out to a family area where we were waiting for him. Donnie ran over laughing and happy to see us.

"How are ya, Don?" Dad said, extending his hand to shake Donnie's. Dad hugged him and patted his back.

"Gimmee five," Michael said.

Michael and Donnie hit hands in the air.

"Gimmee five," I said.

Donnie and I hit hands in the air. Then I bent down to hug him. He stretched his arms out wide and wrapped them tight around my waist, smothering the side of his face in my belly. He searched Dad's face.

"I'm afwaid of da bad lady," Donnie said.

"Who's the bad lady?" I asked.

"Da bad lady comes at night," Donnie said.

"What does she do, Don?" Michael asked.

"I'm afwraid of da bad lady," Donnie said, this time louder.

He didn't tell us what the bad lady did or why she scared him. We made other chit chat. Donnie mentioned the "bad lady" several times more. Dad told him not to make up stories. As we got up to go, Donnie cried and said he was afraid. We left anyway.

Within a few weeks of Donnie's admission, Dorothea visited Dad, demanding to take Donnie out of the Fernald School. She agreed to care for him herself—forever.

She and Bob took Michael and me for visits to their apartment. Donnie had his own bedroom there and a toy box containing his baseball mitt, ball, bat, and his stuffed monkey, "Chadda." We all jumped up and down on his bed.

After dinner, Dorothea drove Michael and me home to our old house with Dad. She brought Donnie back to his new home with her and Bob.

The carpenters finished enough of Eleanor's house addition by 1973 for Dad, Michael, and me to move in. We brought our clothes and my bedroom desk. We left everything else in its place at the old house, dishes in cupboards, food in the fridge, sheets on beds. We walked over our red-white-red kitchen floor, by then chipped and worn, and through the aging wooden door, more scratched and warped than ever.

"What about Rinney?" I said.

"He can live at the garage," Dad said. "I'll feed him."

"I want to take him, too," I said. "Jeff has Gus."

"Well, we'll talk to Eleana. We can come back and get him," Dad said.

At Eleanor's house, I got my own room—Eleanor's old room. Michael shared David's room with him. David was about fifteen. Michael was about fourteen. Randy, who was about sixteen kept his own room, as did Jeff who was about ten.

Kathy, a girl my age, had just moved in next door. A mass of curly orange hair framed Kathy's face. She asserted herself like a young princess. Kathy, too, had twenty-something-year-old siblings, except hers all still lived at home. Kathy's siblings treated her like a little guest, buying her new clothes and commenting about how cute they looked when she tried them on. They talked about what an adorable figure she began developing, warning her about boys in the same breath.

Kathy and I sat up late out on her porch, gossiping about kids at school, gawking at teen stars in *16 Magazine*, and reading about horses. Back at the old house, this was probably about the time mice began ransacking the joint for supplies to build nests and gather stale crumbs for their young. While life was working out for me in my new home, I missed Rinney and worried about him.

A different story unfolded for Michael. My brother had no friends nearby, so after school, he got off the bus at a kid's house a couple miles away and walked home. He asked about doing this often and sometimes Eleanor said he couldn't go. Michael complained to Dad, then resumed his afterschool visits to the friend's house whenever he liked.

Eventually Eleanor quit her telephone company job to stay home with us. The seven of us rubbed elbows around her kitchen table at dinnertime. Dad and Eleanor scolded Michael for talking too loudly or with his mouth full. When I caught Michael's eye at the dinner table, he ignored me—or scowled. He never had to tell me why, though. I knew why. He hated my happiness. We weren't supposed to get a new mother—to be pleased about that. It wasn't loyal to Ma. If he could read my mind as I could read his, he'd recognize I knew there could never be another Ma. Ma was my real mother. She would always be my real mother. The only one who knew I used to pee my bed. I was the only one who watched Ma put on her stockings each morning and clip them to her garter belt. I knew her house dresses hung on the back of our bathroom door—on the inside facing the attic. I knew she sat at our kitchen table sipping from her dainty teacup, looking off into nowhere and using her baby finger for picking her nose. I thought she was the most beautiful woman in the world.

Dinner table conversation at Eleanor's continued.

"Can I please bring Rinney here?" I said.

"Okay, but he must stay outside," said Eleanor.

"I'll build him a doghouse," said Jeff.

The following weekend, Jeffrey salvaged scraps of wood from the yard and used shingles he found inside a dilapidated shed on their property. He constructed a large wooden box big enough for four kids to sit inside. Called it a doghouse. Dad brought Rinney home. We chained him to a tree out by his new house. Eleanor lived on a busy main road, so I didn't chance letting him run loose as he had in my old neighborhood. I went to see him every day. Chains made practicing his tricks harder, so I just fed him and gave him fresh water.

One evening alone in my bedroom, I heard a rumble in the hallway. I opened my door to investigate. David and Michael were wrapped around one another, wrestling. Their faces, red. Their teeth, clenched. Each trying to hold the other back as their feet skidded down the hallway. A fist escaped and sent a blow into Michael's back, another into David's ear. Jeffrey, wearing pajamas and bare feet, also standing in his bedroom doorway, tracked their moves through the lens of a water pistol and squirted them when in good range. Hearing the commotion, Dad rushed upstairs and managed pulling the boys apart. Eleanor came up, one step at a time as she always did and ordered Jeff and me back into our rooms. Dad and Eleanor followed the angry boys into David's room, shut the door. I could hear muted complaining from all four.

Dad and Eleanor went downstairs. I strained to hear their argument. That night Dad and Michael left. Dad returned alone. He said Michael would live with Andy and his wife from then on.

Michael and I had already drifted apart, but now it seemed I'd lost another brother. First Donnie, then Michael. After that, those two came for dinner on Easter, Thanksgiving, and Christmas, then went right back to their respective homes at Dorothea's and Andy's. Dad and Eleanor argued often. My kids this. Your kids that.

It must have been hard for them—these two minds of contrasting origins. Dad, one of eight children, arrived into the world in 1920, just in time for coming of age during the Great Depression. His parents emigrated from Portugal's Madeira Island, traveling through Ellis Island, and somehow winding up in Chelmsford—when most of their Portuguese friends landed in Lowell. His family suffered and scraped through the Depression but managed to keep their home and farm. Dad remembers never having toys or candy as a child—and toiling at farm work before and after school. He left school as a teenager without graduating and started his business at sixteen.

"My friend Earl Kinney broke down, and I hitched his car up to my father's horse and buggy to pull him out. That's how I started out."

He believed in hard work. In my father's world, women stayed home to cook, clean, and care for kids. Men went to work to make money and decisions.

Eleanor was about twelve years younger than Dad. Raised in a working-class home, she grew up in Medford, Massachusetts, a suburb a few miles outside of Boston. Her family fared well during the Depression because her dad had a good job, she said. She had two brothers and spoke of spending summers on Cape Cod with her Aunt Bea. Stricken with polio at fourteen, Eleanor suffered primitive treatments, hundreds of doctor visits, and long hospital stays. It must have been lonely since friends kept away, fearing her contagious. She recovered enough to return home. Graduated from high school with her class in 1950 and took a few classes at Framingham State Teacher's College, but never graduated. The disease left her legs thin and unable to run. She walked with a slight limp. Polio became a part of her identity. In her later years, post-polio syndrome greatly restricted her mobility and physical capabilities. One day years after her divorce, she lost control of her car.

"In those seconds while it flew through the air, I thought, 'This is it,'" she said. "I thought that was the end, but it wasn't. Your father came to tow my car. That's how we met."

She never imagined what other misfortune awaited in getting involved with him. Eleanor taught me how to cut "out," not "off" the core from a head of iceberg lettuce.

Setting tables, she explained, "The blades of knives always go in. When hosting, always say, 'Would you like,' not 'Do you want.'" She said, "Ginger ale is a better choice because it has fewer ('not less') calories than cream soda," which had been my favorite.

My weight dropped. People complimented about how thin I became. Eleanor purchased expensive shampoos and creme rinses to see if we could "get your hair to shine." And it did. I started calling her "Mom." Her relatives sent me cards on my birthdays and brought me souvenirs back from vacations, just like they did for my stepbrothers. I enjoyed ironing shirts, doing dishes, and completing other jobs on the list of chores she left for me on the kitchen table when I got home after school.

While vacuuming our hallway stairs one day, I realized it had been a long while since I asked God for favors. I prayed to let Him know his debt was paid in full. That I didn't need his help anymore. However, if I'd better foresight, I wouldn't have closed our contract so soon.

In Eleanor's neighborhood, it seemed most parents had the right kind of romance at about the same time, bringing to life so many kids within my age range. We all hung out on Kathy's front porch at night, talking, laughing, and learning how to flirt and relax in our awkward bodies and brains. We belonged to each other like a massive kid-family.

Kathy and I sat on her bedroom floor one afternoon with another girl from school, Carolyn, whom I just met. We gossiped about other girls and no doubt, about boys.

Not quite remembering the first part of our conversation, I'm guessing as girls about twelve or thirteen, our usual banter went something like this: "Do you know Kim Collins?" Kathy said, looking at Carolyn.

"Oh yeah, she's a priss," Carolyn said.

"What about Tom Emerson," I said, looking at Carolyn. "Do you know him?"

"Mary has a crush on him," Kathy said.

"No I don't," I said.

"Yeah, I think my brother knows his brother," Carolyn said. "Didn't his father die last year?"

"Yeah," Kathy said. "In a car crash. Such a bummer."

But I remember the second part of our conversion distinctly: Carolyn looked at me, said, "I'm sorry about your mother."

"It's okay," I said.

"Is it true your mother hanged herself?" she said.

I froze. Embarrassed for not knowing how my mother died. I said nothing, wondering if Ma could have done such a thing.

"I'm sorry," she said again.

"Yeah," Kathy said. "That must have been awful."

"It's okay," I repeated, as if I had known all along.

At home later, I mentioned to Eleanor what Carolyn said.

"Didn't you know how your mother died?" she said.

"No, I just knew *that* she died," I said.

Eleanor went into her bedroom. She returned drawing a document from an envelope. "This is your mother's death certificate," she said. She read from the paper, "Asphyxiation by suspension. Mentally deranged."

The words delivered a cold numbness to my chest.

"That's terrible," I said.

I thought back to the morning I came down and told Ma I peed my bed. It seemed by then another world. A lifetime ago. Considering Ma's death with this new information, a magnificent sense of guilt overcame me. Until then, I never knew people could kill themselves that way. Up to that point, I had only heard about hangings from Salem witch trials. Education on savage mobs lynching Black people came later in my life. As a young girl in the north, I hadn't yet heard of such atrocities. Why did Ma punish herself that way? Because I peed my bed? She was "sick and tired of this."

Another time I hurt Ma rushed to mind—about a year before she died during my stay at Saint Joseph's Hospital for a tonsillectomy. Ma visited me as I sat on the children's playroom floor consumed by *Batman and Robin*. I wanted only to watch that show. At home about a week later (they kept patients in hospitals for ten days following tonsillectomies back then), Ma mentioned she felt disappointed because after coming so far to see me, I preferred watching television instead of seeing her. That she'd waited outside in freezing temperatures for Dad to return and get her. As a little girl with Ma still alive, I didn't feel a bit ashamed or guilty about it. After learning how she died, the memory rushed in and hollowed out my heart some more.

"I'm surprised no one told you how she died," said Eleanor. "What did they say when you asked how your mother died?"

"I never asked how she died," I said, feeling ignorant. "She was gone. That was all."

"You people should have all had counseling," she said. "But you know your father."

She meant that Dad's family came from "the old country" as he would say. They considered people who saw therapists to be "Clazy, clazy in the head." Best keep quiet and move on.

For decades, I snuffed out thoughts about Ma's death. Thoughts that tasted like dirty dishwater. I opted instead to worship friends and boys and indulge every little worry and triumph that comes and goes with growing up.

At first, life at Eleanor's seemed good. I spent a lot of time next door at Kathy's hanging out or helping groom her horse. Traipsed around horse shows. Jeff's pony was too small for me. Even without my own horse, I enjoyed watching Kathy and other riders race around barrels and jump fences. I loved petting and cooing at horses and breathing in their aroma—a primal comforting smell, as if from the origins of civilization. An ancient scent from a place I intuitively knew from some distant lifetime it seems.

Jeff and I, with other neighborhood kids, joined a chapter of the 4-H Club for horse lovers, a youth group focusing on agricultural causes. The four Hs stand for head, heart, hands, and health. Leaders demonstrated proper horse care. For those with horses, they conducted unannounced barn inspections, awarding and eliminating points for organization, safety, and cleanliness. The club sponsored horse shows and group rides.

Eleanor said that one day, I would have my own horse in her backyard. At his garage, Dad hoisted the back of a scratched and dented box truck onto his ramp truck, drove across town, unloaded it deep into the woods behind Eleanor's backyard. Dad said when I got my horse, we would use the big box as a barn. Jeff and I bush-whacked our way through a small forest to check it out. As it turned out, I never had a horse in that backyard. Just as I thought everything would be ok—that settled in a new family, the era of chaos ended—things turned wild again.

At dinner one night with Eleanor, Dad, and her boys, Eleanor bumped her cup and spilled hot tea on her lap. Dad laughed.

"You son of a bitch," she screamed at him.

"That's an awful thing for you to say about my motha," he said, pointing a finger at her. "I'm goin' back to work."

He walked out and slammed the door, leaving our walls quivering behind him.

Later that evening, I heard their raised voices again. Within my bedroom walls, I couldn't discern their words—just noise. His inconsiderate defense noise. Her trying to teach an incorrigible man a lesson noise.

This was about the time my bedroom ceiling in our old empty house began to leak, sending a thin stream of water behind the wallpaper like a river on a map, flowing diagonally down over its terrain.

Next day after school, Eleanor said she was sick of "your father's" inconsideration. That she enjoyed my presence. But he made her miserable. She complained about Dad's relatives "that tribe over there; can't even buy a hankie without them all knowing it." She said Dorothea "made her own bed, taking Donnie like that." She said my aunties, my mother's sisters, had no business getting upset because she took me into a Protestant church.

"I didn't know they were upset about that," I said.

"At least I'm taking you to church," she shrieked.

On and on and on and on, she went. I listened, nodding in agreement. Dad returned that evening. We ate dinner together as though nothing extraordinary happened the night before.

Decades later as a grown woman, I discovered they weren't slinging hatred toward one another, but distress signals. All she needed was for him to say, "I'm sorry; I'll try harder." And then for him to do just that. But Dad was "set in his ways" as she often said. He lived in his home like a businessman lives in a hotel room. Home had always been simply a place for him to rest and refuel, and to one day find his children grown and released into the wilds of society, surviving on their own. As a child, I secretly sided with Dad. His misogyny seemed as certain a condition of life as traffic lights on the way to school. I wanted Eleanor to amend *her* ways to bring peace to our lives. So programmed was I to accept Dad *as is*, I didn't perceive his responsibility to meet her halfway.

The weather turned cold. Evening weathermen predicted single digit temperatures at night. Jeff and I, about thirteen by this time, begged to bring our dogs inside. Eleanor said Gus could come in because as a beagle, he didn't have enough fur to keep himself warm. Rinney, she said, had plenty of fur—he could stay outside.

"That ain't fair," I said.

"There's no such word as ain't. Say isn't," she corrected me.

"That isn't fair," I repeated.

Next morning, I went outside to check on Rinney.

"Rinney," I called as I crunched through snow toward his doghouse. He didn't come running out wagging his tail. "Rinney." As I came nearer, I saw him, lying in snow. I knelt down, pet him. His body felt as hard as ice, frozen solid. This mixture of guilt and deep disappointment rushed through my veins. I felt it burn everywhere, my face, my head, my chest, my arms, my stomach, my legs, my feet.

I floated back toward the house, opened the back door to bacon sizzling and screamed, "Rinney froze to death."

"Shoulda let him in last night," Dad said to no one person in particular.

"Well, I thought he'd be okay," said Eleanor. "Jeffrey, you'll have to bury him when it's warmer."

There were no hugs. No "I'm sorrys." No place to put the pain, the guilt. I wish I could say I ran to my room, buried my face in a pillow, and moped around for a month, but that's not how my young brain handled it. That afternoon, I went to Kathy's, told her I found Rinney frozen in snow "as dead as a doornail," quoting Dickens. She howled in laughter and repeated my words. Everything seemed hilarious between us two. We joked about it during my remaining visit there that day. However, beneath my joyous facade, I seethed.

Soon Eleanor started dropping me off at Saint Anthony's Church on Sundays, so I could prepare for confirmation, one of seven Catholic sacraments. Confirmation "confirms" baptism. It teaches a process for repenting sins and accepting accountability for bad behavior. Days leading up to the event, I learned to confess my sins to a priest and memorize the *Act of Contrition*, a prayer expressing sorrow for wrongdoing and asking for God's forgiveness. On a weekday afternoon before confirmation, I entered the confession box for the first time.

Made of wood carved in fancy designs, the box stood slightly smaller than a gas station attendant booth. I lifted the heavy maroon drape and stepped inside. Slid the drape shut, and knelt on the kneeler, as we practiced doing in Sunday school. Darkness. I waited. The priest, kneeling opposite me, slid a small wooden window open, revealing only his wrinkled face in blackness behind a screen.

I blessed myself, making the sign of the cross over my body by first touching my forehead, then my chest, my left shoulder, my right shoulder. I held my hands together in prayer position and whispered "Bless me Father for I have sinned. This is my first confession."

I confessed the usual. Swearing, acting unkind, not helping enough at home. I did not confess I sent my mother to her grave by wetting my bed. I kept all that to myself.

The priest whispered the traditional prayer in response, "God, the Father of mercies, through the death and resurrection of his Son has reconciled the world to himself and sent the Holy Spirit among us for the forgiveness of sins. Through the ministry of the Church may God give you pardon and peace. I absolve you from your sins in the name of the Father, and of the Son, and of the Holy Spirit. Go say one *Our Father* and two *Hail Marys* as your penance."

I left hoping that covered everything, including the sins I didn't confess out loud. On Sunday, March 25, 1973, my entire family gathered for my confirmation at the church as if we were one big happy bunch. Confirmation girls wore a white garment draped over our clothes, like a graduation gown, and a red beanie hat. I don't remember what boys wore—a blue gown and beanie?

The ritual required me to choose another godparent, besides Uncle Sonny and Auntie Jeannie, whom Ma had chosen for me as a baby. I chose Dorothea. During the ceremony, Dorothea stood behind me, placing her hand on my shoulder as is customary.

The bishop rubbed Chrism (holy) oil on my forehead and said a prayer, "Be sealed with the gift of the Holy Spirt."

I responded, "Amen."

Then he said, "Peace be with you."

I responded, "Also with you."

We all went to dinner after the ceremony—Dad, Eleanor, Dorothea, Bob, Donnie, Michael, Randy, David, and Jeff. At a restaurant, Eleanor handed me a heavy box wrapped in white paper, white ribbon, and a white bow. Tearing the paper off, I discovered a white Bible inside. Dorothea handed me a little box wrapped in white paper. A tiny white bow perched on top. I scratched tape from the bottom, then tore off its wrapping to reveal a small black box. I lifted its cover against the slight resistance of its tiny metal hinges. Tucked in white satin was a thin gold band. A tiny diamond set within a teardrop-shaped onyx stone.

"That's the diamond Ma saved for you," Dorothea said.

Placing the ring on my ring finger, I held it out and admired it, remembering Ma taking down that little juice glass containing the tissue paper, picking at the paper, and showing me the sparkling stone.

Chapter 5

Still early springtime, Dad stood against a counter with his arms folded across his chest. Eleanor sat at the table, crying.

"Mary Gayle," he said. "Get your clothes and books for school. We're leaving."

"Where are we going?" I asked.

"The old house," he said. "We're not welcome here anymore."

"I didn't say that," said Eleanor.

Dad's darting eyes and pouting conveyed he needed me to hustle. I hurried to my room, scanned the clutter for essentials. Books, underwear, my favorite jeans, shirts. Something to carry them in? I ripped the pillowcase off my pillow and threw the items in. Dad waited outside in his red Cadillac.

"Dad, what happened?" I asked, once in the car.

"I can't live wit that woman," he said. "She goes on and on. Doesn't know when to stop. All she does is com-plaiaiaiaiain, com-plaiaiaiaiain, com-plaiaiaiaiain."

We drove the remaining distance in silence.

At our old house, the worn wooden door creaked its, "Oh brother; they're back" as Dad and I walked in. Everything appeared as we left it about two years ago, albeit for a coating of dust. The red-white-red kitchen floor. Ma's pantry. Her cookbooks. The padded wooden chair where Dad sat at nighttime. The tattered green sofa beside it. Dad went into the basement to turn on the heat, while I stood in the kitchen, not sure what to do. He came back upstairs, said it would warm up soon. Then he left for his garage next door.

I stood alone in that kitchen, still thinking of my next step. Lifted our telephone receiver. Still heard a dial tone. Hooked the receiver back on the wall mount.

In my old bedroom, I stood in the doorway. Noticed the water stain left during winter, its crooked line running from a ceiling corner to halfway down my faded pink wallpaper. On my floor, the mass of papers and books I'd stacked there while cleaning out my desk for its trip to my new bedroom. Mice turds everywhere. A magazine featuring a picture of David Cassidy, a tween pop culture superstar who now repulsed me. My unmade bed, its mismatched sheets, pillowcase, and blankets, as I'd left them years earlier. I lay on my cold bed, still wearing my jacket. Freezing and displaced, I closed my eyes, fell asleep. Awoke in darkness to the door downstairs squealing open. Walked down. Dad placed a gallon of milk into our refrigerator.

"I brought you a chicken parm sub from George's," he said.

I thanked him. Ate it.

He ate his meatball sub or Italian grinder or whatever it was without talking. He crumbled the white wrapper, tossed it into the garbage.

"I'm goin' ta bed," he said.

He went upstairs to his bed. I went up to mine. I lay there in my clothes until I fell back asleep. Next day, a Sunday, I walked over to Dad's garage next door. Of course I had better things to do. Could have written poems, cleaned the house, called Kathy. But the shock and uncertainty smothered all passion. Cutting across a path in a small field on the way over, I could hear Dad banging something. *Clang! Clang! Clang!*

Dad could always be found at this garage on Sundays and all other days of the week. He didn't take Sundays off because to him, working felt better than sitting through Mass. He attended church for only funerals and weddings. Yet, his church prevailed as the parish in which we'd learn our prayers, marry, and bless our dead.

"I talked to the priest," Dad often said. "He said I worked so hard I don't needa go-ta church."

Dad remained convinced his hard work earned him a private dispensation from the Vatican, allowing him to miss Mass without sin for the rest of his life. No doubt Dad worked hard, but his garage was also his happy place—where men communed. Besides Uncle Johnny, whose house sat opposite Dad's garage, you could bump into any number of guys there on a given day. Local policemen, the mailman, neighbors, older cousins, town workers, and Dad's friends: Johnny Jason, Henry Divine, Earl Kinney, and another he only referred to as John-the-Raker. Dad hid Miller Lights in the free space inside his Coke machine. On warm summer nights, he and the guys stood amid compressors, tire rods, fenders plastered in pink putty, and boxes of motor oil, sipping beer, recalling days gone by.

"Remember that time Flying A sent us kites to give away with gas?" Dad said.

Flying A was a brand of gasoline Dad sold in the sixties.

"Yeah, and we tried a few out?" said Uncle Johnny.

"Do you know it came out in the goddamned newspaper that all we do around here all day is fly goddamned kites," Dad said, now looking at his laughing cohort.

"What I wanna know is who the hell took those goddamned pichas and sent 'em ta-da paypa?" Dad said.

As I entered his garage that Sunday, Dad, wearing his green work uniform, sat on an upside-down dirty white plastic bucket. His mind fixated on a brake pad. He smacked the wheel using a miniature sledgehammer, whacking it harder each time. *Clang! Clang! CLANG!*

I managed yelling over the noise, "Hey Dad, got any jobs I can do?"

He turned, glanced at me, turned back around to the car, and pounded three more times. *CLANG! CLANG! CLANG!* Probably harder due to his frustration over what to do with this teenage girl standing in his workplace. He dropped his hammer and looked back at me. Maybe he was hoping I'd disappeared. I must have been such an inconvenience. All his life, he worked hard to prevent the poverty he'd known as a child. While he prepared to avoid financial crisis, he never expected struggling as a single dad.

"Why don't ya clean them tools on that bench," he said, pointing toward his metal bench piled high with sockets, pliers, wrenches, metal files, a crowbar, chisels, and an assortment of hammers, large and small.

"You can use this," he said, passing me a grease-stained rag. "Just wipe 'em down."

44

I dug in, lifting one heavy instrument after another, using the rag for wiping each off. This effort wasn't making any difference. I went into the bathroom. In Dad's white soapstone sink, grayed from years of grime and splattered in grease-stained blemishes, I wet the cloth, and shook out some Boraxo on it. That's a coarse powdered soap Dad used for handwashing. I grabbed a long swath of paper towel from a jumbo roll hanging from the ceiling. Back at Dad's bench, I scrubbed tools with the soapy cloth, then a dry paper towel.

Eleanor pulled up in her maroon station wagon. I stayed in back, wiping tools. Dad's office door creaked open—and clicked shut. A few minutes later, the door creaked open again. They said quiet goodbyes, followed by a long silence. Then she emerged from the office, got into her car, and drove away.

"Tonight, we're goin' back ta Eleana's," he said when he returned. "Dinner is at six o'clock."

It seemed a relief returning to the place that had become home. To my bedroom sanctuary, to friends I made. Done cleaning a good number of tools, I washed my hands in that dirty sink and headed back to the old house. Packed my clothes and schoolbooks back into my pillowcase, and scanned my room, considering if anything else should come. No, nothing.

I pushed the doorknob button-lock in, closed the wooden door, and hid our key above an emergency switch in the entry hallway. Outside, paint had begun bubbling on the house siding.

That evening, we had dinner at Eleanor's as if nothing strange happened.

Before too long though, Dad and Eleanor had another blowout, and he and I returned to our old, cold house again. Next day, they made up. We returned to her place. Dad saw Michael every day since Andy lived a few houses away from Dad's garage—and Michael could walk over to the garage after school. But I still saw Michael, Donnie, and my other siblings only at Christmastime and other major holidays.

Kathy and I spent countless afternoons sitting on her bedroom floor, doing homework, and listening to records, like *Hair*, by The Cowsills. We'd sing our favorite verses, looking at each other and smiling as we did.

"I met a new guy at Cindy's house," said Kathy. Kathy babysat for Cindy.

She told me about a boy, Wallace, whom she liked, but thought I'd like even more since she technically still dated Ricky Hines in our group.

"Can I give him your number?" Kathy asked.

"Eleanor will flip out if a boy calls me," I said.

"Okay, well, I'll give you his number," Kathy said. "Will that work?"

"I guess so," I said.

She scrawled a number on a corner of white lined paper, tore it off, handed it over.

"This is Cindy's number; he is always over there because his best friend Jesse is her brother. Jesse lives at Cindy's" she explained. This innocent gesture between two teenage friends eventually invited greater dysfunction into my life.

I stuffed the paper into the front pocket of my jeans.

To alleviate overcrowding at our junior high school that year, Chelmsford Public School administrators split our school day into two sessions. Kathy and I had afternoon sessions, which meant our bus came at about noon. In wintertime the sky turned black by the time we got home. Once Dad and Eleanor left for work, I pretty much had the house to myself before school.

One early spring morning before school, Kathy and I sat in our family room, the one with the wall-to-wall fireplace. Jeff joined us. He was supposed to go to school. Patrick, a neighborhood boy I had a crush on, showed up. We chatted, smoked cigarettes, decided on skipping school altogether that day. Kathy left to change clothes, saying she'd come back later. Patrick, Jeff, and I continued smoking and laughing, reveling in our run of the house and freedom. Until Dad pulled up. As it turned out, he attended a meeting that morning, which required a suit. He came home to change into work clothes.

We scrambled to put out our cigarettes in the fireplace. The door down the hall creaked open. Jeff ran out. His feet sprinted past Dad, upstairs, and into his bedroom where his door clicked shut. Dad's footsteps strolled down the hall. Patrick and I stared wide-eyed at each other over the smoky haze.

"What's goin' on?" Dad said. His steel wool eyebrows slanted downward.

"We're just hanging out, Dad," I said.

"Who's smokin' cigarettes?" he asked.

I just looked at him. Said nothing. Frightened.

"Who are you?" Dad said, looking at Patrick. "You betta get the hell outta here."

Patrick got up and started walking past him.

"Were you smokin' cigarettes?" Dad asked as he walked by.

Patrick ignored him and walked out of the house.

Dad turned his anger toward me.

"I don't have time-ta deal with you right now," he said, pointing a finger at me. "I have-ta get back-ta the garage." He left the room and returned a few minutes later wearing his green work uniform.

"Wait 'til ya motha gets home tonight," he said. Then he walked out, got into his Cadillac, and drove away.

Panicked, I ran over to Kathy's.

"I can't go home," I said. "They will kill me."

"You are screwed," she agreed.

"I need to run away," I said.

"Where will you go?" she said.

"I'll hitchhike as far as I can go," I said.

"I'll make you a peanut butter sandwich," she said. "And we can pack some carrots, too."

She thought I was joking. To Kathy, it seemed just another one of our adventures. To her, we were *making believe* I was running away. As we smothered bread in peanut butter and chopped up carrots, Kathy sang The Beatles' "She's Leaving Home."

We bagged up the sandwiches and carrots. Kathy stuffed them into my jacket pockets. We walked down her driveway toward the road.

"Bye," I said, walking up busy Groton Road toward Westford.

"Bye," she said, smiling and waving, lifting her hand way above her head as if I just boarded the Titanic and she was standing on shore, wishing me a bon voyage. My friend still thought we were just pretending about my running away.

Early spring temperatures left large puddles on the side of the road. Tires swooshed through, splashing and dirtying shrunken snowbanks. The air smelled of fresh earth. I walked and walked and walked and walked and walked the few miles into Westford. As cars zoomed by, I turned around, stuck out my thumb. Imagined finding a hippie commune where I could do chores and live. A man driving a brown El Camino, which is like half car, half pickup truck, stopped.

"Need a ride?" he asked.

"No, I'm good," I replied. Something about him frightened me. Maybe it was the whistle in his voice, like he was part weasel. Maybe it was how his eyes assessed me up and down. Whatever it was, I didn't want to get in.

With his car gone, I turned around, began again walking and walking and walking, then walking backwards holding my thumb out. Soon afterward the same guy cruised by me. He disappeared. I ran, crouched behind a stone wall, and imagined hearing his car again. After a short while, I stood and began walking backwards again with my thumb up. By this time, I made it to Shirley, about five miles from Eleanor's house in North Chelmsford. The sky turned orange. My hands, cold.

A man driving a large four-door sedan stopped. He seemed decent, well-mannered, so I hopped in. His car felt warm. Smelled like spearmint gum. It was a relief resting after so much walking.

"Where are you headed?" he asked.

"Just up the road," I said.

"Where are you from?" he asked.

"North Chelmsford," I said.

"What's a young girl like you doing hitchhiking?" he asked. "Don't you know how dangerous it can be?"

I shrugged.

"You are running away, aren't you?" he asked.

I didn't reply.

"Listen, I know a nice family who will take you in," he said. "Let me take you over there."

"Okay," I said.

He drove me to a large triple decker house in Worcester, located about a fifty-minute drive from North Chelmsford. I didn't know it then but, back then Worcester was a rundown city renowned for drug trafficking. We got out of his car, climbed several stone steps toward the front door of the multi-family house. He knocked. A petite woman wearing long, grey French curls and a tall, thin man with salt and pepper hair answered the door. They stared at the man, then at me. The couple invited us in and introduced me to their daughter who was my age. The man and the couple sat at the kitchen table and whispered while the daughter and I played board games on the living room carpet. Her little brother, who was about five, sat beside us, begging to play, too.

Their apartment in that large house contained two bedrooms. The girl had her own tidy pink bedroom. Her brother had a bed in their parents' room. Once the grownups were done talking, the man who brought me there mentioned I could stay with these people. Then he left. The couple asked me to come sit at the table. The woman asked if I was hungry and dumped a can of SpaghettiOs in a saucepan. Eleanor would be appalled, I thought.

I later learned that at home, Dad and Eleanor called Kathy, looking for me. Kathy told them I ran away. I can imagine the conversation.

"She ran away, and you didn't tell anyone?" Eleanor likely said.

"I didn't think she would really do it," Kathy likely replied.

"Do you know where she ran away to?" they probably asked.

"She went toward Westford," Kathy might have said.

The woman placed the bowl of warmed pasta in front of me and asked if I wanted to talk about "it." I explained what happened that day—the skipping school, the boy, the cigarettes, how I felt afraid to go home.

Meanwhile, Dad called the Chelmsford Police Department who sent a detective to the house. Dad explained how he found me at home smoking cigarettes with a boy. They were probably discussing how I got out of hand and needed reining in.

At the table before my SpaghettiOs, the couple welcomed me to stay overnight, but only under the condition I call home the next day. I agreed. Meanwhile at home, the detective searched my bedroom for a note and other clues about my whereabouts. He found a note scrawled in my handwriting, hole-punched on top, and hung from a single strand of yellow yarn threaded through the hole and taped onto the bookshelf above my desk. He probably rushed toward it, grabbed it, read it—then felt disappointed in seeing only my list of homework assignments and no clues about where I went or why I fled.

That evening, the girl and I stayed up and talked about school and friends and boys. At bedtime, the girl and the woman said to sleep in the girl's room. That the girl would sleep on the couch. The girl insisted she loved sleeping on the couch.

As I lay awake, it was the first time that day I considered my family might be worried about me. That they may think I was dead in a ditch somewhere. That even though I had a crazy family—I still had a family. A tear rolled down my cheek as I fell into a deep sleep.

Next morning, the father took the girl, her brother, and me to Friendly's Restaurant for pancakes.

"We'll have breakfast. Then you must call your family on that pay phone," he said, turning around and pointing to a pay phone on the corner wall near some restrooms. I saw the phone, mounted within its brown wooden case. A thick book of yellow pages hung by a metal cord from the shelf below it. He explained I could stay longer, or he would bring me home that day, again, under one condition. I must let my family know I was safe.

"Okay," I said.

We finished eating. The waitress cleared our plates. The man slid a dime across the table. My stomach tightened. He pointed to the phone. I walked over, dropped the dime into the slot on top, waited for the dial tone, and punched in the number. It rang half a ring.

"Hello?" Eleanor said.

"Hi," I said.

"Mary Gayle, I'm so glad to hear your voice," she giggled. "Are you all right?"

I explained where I was. She said she and Dad wanted me home. That they loved me and missed me. I told her about the nice family who took me in. That they would bring me home that afternoon.

Calling released pressure inside my chest. Perhaps we could hit *reset* on our relationships. I would try behaving. Maybe Dad and Eleanor would stop fighting. The man returned to their apartment for his wife. Then we drove the fifty minutes toward Eleanor's house. An unfamiliar car sat in the driveway. I later learned that vehicle belonged to the detective. Embraced by warm thoughts of my phone call home and guarded by my new family, I wasn't afraid to face Dad and Eleanor following the incident in the living room with the boy and cigarettes the previous morning.

We all walked in together, the couple, their children, and me. The detective rushed the couple off to a corner in our hallway. He began interrogating them as their children, serious and as still as sculptures, stared. "Do you know it's wrong holding a minor? Have you had any contact with her before? Why did you wait a day before calling ..." and on and on. The couple appeared terrified.

"We would never harm her," said the woman. "We were trying to help. We love her."

At that, Eleanor let loose, "You love her? You don't even know her," she shrieked. "How can you love her?"

"She's been through a lot," the woman said.

"She's been through a lot?" Eleanor said. "We have been through a heck of a lot more than her."

Dad looked on, holding his arms folded across his chest as if watching an event unfold on the street among strangers, not his own family.

The detective advised the couple that if they ever tried contacting me in any way at all, they would be arrested. Then the couple and their children bolted out the door.

I never saw or heard from them again. But countless times as an adult, I felt fortunate for landing with them that day, and not with some lunatic who raped me and ripped out my slaughtered guts on the side of some closed off road. I'm also grateful I had parents, as wild and weird as things were, who cared enough to try finding me. I'm sorry now I put them through that. It would take me a good many years to grow into these conclusions. As a young teen, my brain was still soft baked and struggling, steeped in instability.

Chapter 6

Rather than easing up, Dad and Eleanor's clashes intensified. I thought about the boy, Wallace, Kathy told me about. One night with no one else home, I dialed the number on the crumpled paper I had stuffed into my jeans. Wallace sounded happy to hear from me. Soon he hung out with us on Kathy's porch. Before I knew it, we kissed goodnight in the shadow of a tree between Eleanor's and Kathy's houses. It had to have been about 1974. I was fourteen. He was seventeen. White shoulder-length hair. Steely blue eyes. His red face made him always look embarrassed.

Sneaking out, I saw him whenever I could. Our favorite hideaway became the top of a retaining wall under a highway bridge located down the road from Eleanor's house. While cars sped just a few feet above us, we sat cuddled under the bridge beams, kissing, talking for hours.

Before long, Dad and Eleanor blew up again and again and again. Back and forth into and out of the old house we went—for a day or two each time. Just long enough to toss up home and school life into a confetti of confusion. The last time must have been by about 1976. A police officer came because Dad threatened leaving with a new television he purchased. Eleanor demanded the tube stay at her house. The police officer turned out to be one of Dad's friends.

Dad laughed and said, "She's ova-reactin'."

The policeman didn't laugh, though. Dad said he'd leave the television. The policeman stood in the doorway.

"Mary Gayle, c'mon, we're leavin'," Dad said.

"Wait," Eleanor said. "It's not fair for her—going back and forth all the time. Her friends are here."

"What-da wanna do?" Dad asked, looking at me.

"Stay?" I said.

"Fine," Dad said. He rushed past the policeman and left. The policeman followed.

I felt detached. First, I lost Ma, then my siblings, now Dad. Like Ma used to say, "Nobody owns me." But here I had friends. I had Wallace. I had Eleanor's guidance, but our relationship grew strained.

Weeks went by. Then months. No Dad.

Eleanor grounded me for talking "flip." I rolled my eyes, walked away.

As an adult now witnessing fiery relationships between my friends and their daughters, I wonder how much of the commotion between her and me developed out of my own feral spirit. Did I push further due to the insanity around me? Maybe. But analysis of how much of my naughtiness originated from one cause or another hides in the messiness of dysfunction and parent–child relations.

In my bedroom during this detention one night about a week later, I heard a *tick-tick-tick* in rapid succession on my window. I looked out. Kathy stood down there next to Ricky Hines and a boy I didn't know. I opened my window. They had thrown pebbles at it to get my attention.

"What are you guys doing?" I whispered.

"Come out with us," she said.

"I'm grounded," I said.

"Oh well, I can throw one of these up to you," she said, lifting her jean jacket to reveal a shiny silver can of beer.

After Kathy's many failed tries at throwing it up to my second-floor window, I tied several pairs of panty hose together and sent the drop line down. This adventure meant more to us than the beer. It was never about the beer. But beer made it surreptitious. Exciting. She wrapped and wrapped and tied the can in the hose. I hoisted it up. I managed reeling the can all the way up. We giggled until our bellies were sore. Then she slipped away into blackness. I didn't want to drink it, but figured, what the heck and popped the top.

Next day, I came home from school. Eleanor, furious, sat at the kitchen table, waiting for me. My empty beer sat crushed and propped up before her.

"I found *this* in your room," she yelled and slapped my face. I felt ashamed, believing then and still now that I deserved that whack. "What are you doing drinking beer in my house?" she screamed. "After all I do for you?"

David tiptoed by carrying a handful of cookies and a glass of milk, as if walking through a church service. Stairs creaked. Then his bedroom door clicked shut. Jeff, swaying back and forth in his favorite rocking chair, watched the scene unfurl from the hallway as if watching an episode of *MASH* on television.

My chest fired up with worry.

"While your father is over there without a care in the world!" she yelled. "I've had enough. I must go to work. It will make me late, but I'm taking you back to your father's right now. Get your things."

Terrified, I rushed upstairs, pitched as much as I could get into a pillowcase, grabbed schoolbooks, and met her outside in her maroon station wagon.

"That's the thanks I get," she said.

She shifted into reverse, raced backward, and sped toward the onramp for Route 3 South. She stared straight ahead, both hands tight on the wheel. Speeding.

"I tried to do the right thing. What do you do?" she screamed. "You act like a brat! That's what!"

I studied a tear in the foot mat.

She exited the highway, sped around a rotary, flew down a ramp on the other side. "Why do I bother? Why? Because I'm stupid. A fool! That's why," she screamed, still looking straight ahead, as if talking to herself.

The tear's fringe edges had blackened—dirt gathered in the fray.

"I thought he'd come back for your sake," she yelled. "But no, not him."

Beyond torn, the tattered material was actually a hole, worn from years of pressure borne down on it. No doubt, the unraveling would continue. We lurched forward as she stopped at a red light.

"He pawned you off on me. Michael off on Andy. Donnie off on Dorothea. Now he's over there. No one to worry about but himself," she exploded.

"What happens when I rub my foot over the hole?" I thought.

Eleanor accelerated.

"Well, he's in for a big surprise today!" she said.

Using the tip of my shoe, I tried making all the hole's fringe-parts go in one direction.

Couldn't.

"You're making me late for work," she shrieked, accentuating the word *work* with increased acceleration on the gas.

Eleanor raced up the driveway to Dad's garage, braked hard, jerking us forward. Framed by the wide opening of his big bay door, Dad held a hand on his forehead to block sun as he watched us. I scampered out, clutching my pillowcase and books. Dad stared as Eleanor dropped me off and zoomed away.

He turned to me. "What happened?" he asked.

I looked up at him and a tide of tears flooded in.

Chapter 7

Dad brought me to Dorothea and Bob's. They'd had a baby, Todd, and by this time, rented a small, two-bedroom cape—or did it have three bedrooms?—from Uncle Johnny, located a few houses down from the old house. Rather than staying at the old house, Dad had been sleeping in his motor home parked behind his garage.

"She can stay here with us," Dorothea said.

"Where will she sleep?" Dad asked.

"In Donnie's room," Dorothea said. "Is that okay, Donnie?"

"Yeah," said Donnie, chuckling. "Meg-gayle can stay in my room." We all laughed.

"It's settled then," Dorothea said.

Donnie's room had slanted ceilings on both sides. Dorothea gave me his bed. He seemed happy with a mattress on the floor—like this was some kind of slumber party.

Soon after I moved in, Dorothea mentioned Eleanor had checked into Solomon Mental Health Center hospital. I felt guilty, like I caused her admission. Still, I was afraid to see her again—to experience another family implosion. Over the next week, I saw Kathy only at school. We were in our last year of junior high school.

"Why did you leave?" she asked. "Your stepmother wants you and your father back. Jeff is really upset."

"I can't, Kathy," I explained. "I'm not happy there."

"Ever think of anyone else's happiness?" she asked and walked away.

My Spanish teacher led me out to the hallway one day. He had called my home because my grades were slipping.

"I talked with your stepmother," he said.

My face went hot.

"She said you didn't live there anymore," he said. "She was very sad. You should consider going back."

As if I could fix her and Dad's problems. I didn't respond. Next day, Dad got a request from my guidance counselor for a meeting among us three—Dad, the guidance counselor, and me. We sat on plastic chairs in such tight quarters our knees nearly touched. She asked about my low grades. Dad explained it had been a rough year.

"I need a woman in my life," he said, like he forgot this was about me. "It's not workin'," he went on.

The guidance counselor looked at Dad like a mother observes her sick child.

"Dad, I don't want Eleanor doing what Ma did," I said.

Dad studied his shoes and cried big sobs. Then he pulled out his handkerchief and wiped his nose. This was the one and only time he and I discussed losing Ma. My one-way sentence. His sobs. We left that day without a strategy. We didn't speak while driving home, but a new silent peace grew between us.

At home, Dorothea seemed grateful gaining a helper to watch Todd and Donnie when she ran out for errands. Despite missing my friends, I felt great relief. Doing dishes together one night, she asked "So what happened?'

"Eleanor is upset because I have been doing bad things," I confessed.

"Like what?" asked Dorothea.

"Smoking cigarettes," I said. I didn't mention drinking beer and running away and kissing a boy under a highway bridge. Nor did I mention Dad's multiple departures.

Dorothea, Bob, and I discussed life at Eleanor's over cigarettes and tea at night. That's when I explained about the back and forth to and from the old house and the wild ride to Dad's garage. Dorothea mentioned Jackie had lived at their house for a while.

"He's been clean since before getting married," said Bob.

I didn't call Wallace during this time. My old neighborhood teemed with aunties and uncles—a set of them in every household. Someone in this family village would discover and report our relationship to Dad. I feared what he would do and say. So I let Wallace go. Still, I needed something to do.

Dad kept two retired standardbred racehorses, Red's Bonnie Mac and Louie Yates, at a barn and corral behind his garage. A chestnut mare, Bonnie was about six years old. She stood solid and round. Despite her dusty fur, her coat shone like velvet after brushing.

Standing beside me by his corral gate, Dad watched the chestnut mare and warned, "Be careful near her. Them guys at the barn worked her for months. She didn't take ta-da sulky. She just reared up and pulled away. Broke the reins and everythin'. They gave up on her."

"Hi Bonnie," I whispered. She bobbed up and down over to me. I scratched her neck and she nuzzled against me. I climbed between horizontal fence posts and went inside and stroked her neck.

"Careful," Dad said.

Louie, the dark bay about twenty years old, plodded over. Years ago, as a trotter, this big guy won Dad many trophies and ribbons and God knows how much money. Louie had always sniffed Ma's handbag for the sugar cubes she carried just for him. I pulled a couple of carrots from a pocket, held them out, one for each horse. They crunched away.

After that, I walked over to see them every day after school. Louie's coat grew in shabbier than Bonnie's. I knew Dad fed him every day. Still, his ribs were showing. Their manes and tails were knotted. No one had picked their hoofs in years. Learning horse care from the 4-H Club, I knew how to help them.

My new home with Dorothea and Bob sat as far away from Eleanor's house as possible without leaving town. Kids in my old neighborhood attended a different junior high school, but Dad said I could stay at my same school. He or one of his employees drove me in each day. Sometimes Uncle Johnny gave me a ride to Kathy's on weekends. I didn't see Jeff or Eleanor. Kathy and I entered Chelmsford High School that fall and grew apart. Most of our friends chose a technical high school in another town. I never got to say goodbye to them all—they just disappeared. Kathy began hanging out with a new group—theater kids.

Dad took me to the tack shop for horse grooming supplies. I chose two types of brushes, along with a wire mane and tail comb, a hoof pick, some Bag Balm, a leadline, and other grooming supplies. Dad stored hay and grain in a tack room beside his barn. A tattered racing sulky covered in cobwebs stood against a wall. A harness blotched in mildew hung beside it. I swept out that tack room and organized my new supplies in there, hanging them on rusty nails. I took a brush and approached Bonnie. I held it to her nose. She sniffed. Then I began brushing her neck. She leaned into my brush as if enjoying its course scratch on her itchy neck. She stood as still as stone for me—except her tail, busy swatting flies. I patted her rump as I walked around her backside, just as I had learned to do. Then I teased out knots from her mane and tail using the wire comb. Picked and cleaned each of her hoofs, noticing they needed a trim. Dabbed a bit of Bag Balm on her scratches. That ritual over, I approached Louie holding the brush out. He walked away. I figured perhaps he felt peaceful living his remaining days without preening. Dad agreed to having a blacksmith over to trim their hooves and give them shoes.

At dinner, Dad, Dorothea, and Bob hatched a plan to renovate the old house into two apartments—one upstairs for Dad, me, and Michael and another downstairs for Bob, Dorothea, Todd, and Donnie. Soon contractors tore down Ma's knotty pine paneling from kitchen walls. They tore out Ma's pantry and red-white-red kitchen floor. A new linoleum floor and barn board walls were installed. Contractors set new cabinets and drawers into place. Re-did the ceilings and all the rest. The den with the television and the lumpy green sofa became a dining room with a built-in china cabinet and bay window.

Upstairs, three new rooms were added onto the house front, a kitchen, a living room, and a bedroom above it. Carpenters demolished the bathroom where I washed my dollies' hair. They renovated that space into a new bedroom of brown paneled walls for Michael. They built two small bathrooms upstairs—one for me, one for Michael and Dad, where the boys' old bedroom had been. Dad took the room he and

Ma had shared, after replacing wallpaper, carpeting, and furniture, and arranging his bed and chests differently than how he and Ma had them. I got to keep what had always been my childhood bedroom. Dad made good on a promise for its new wallpaper, flooring, and window. At a wallpaper store, I chose a landscape of trees and fields, imagining it a place where I'd like to ride Bonnie someday.

"That design is used in hallways, not bedrooms," said the clerk.

"That's okay," Dad said. "She can get whateva she wants. It's for her room. She has-ta live wit it."

We chose carpeting and light fixtures. In the living room, a carpenter built a full-size liquor bar covered in fire-engine-red shag carpet. Dad chose gold wallpaper and carpet. He purchased a voluptuous gold sofa, matching chairs, an ornately carved Mediterranean coffee table, and matching side tables. Large lamps adorned in shiny gold leaves topped the tables.

"This place looks like a scene out of a mob movie," Dorothea said.

She and Bob designed a more traditional brick and barn board style apartment.

At night, instead of going to horseracing or "up the track" as he called it, Dad stayed home. He and I sanded new kitchen cabinets together. We stained and varnished them while Dorothea and Bob finished theirs downstairs as well. Once the varnish dried, we rubbed the wood using a fine steel wool and varnished them again until they were as smooth as glass. We toiled in near silence, talking about only the work at hand. I sensed a quiet awareness of our common purpose in building a new life.

"Where's Michael?" I said, solely to point out he wasn't there helping us.

"He's in his room, holdin' down his bed," Dad replied.

It was a prouder place with those renovations. Yet there was something regrettable about them, too. These updates destroyed what remained of the beloved features I'd treasured as a child. The upstairs bathroom. The landing at the bottom of the stairs. Ma's red and white checkerboard floor. Her guardhouse. Still, the old house remained the familiar friend I knew, like a person who grows up and goes off to college, but deep down still doesn't change. However, our relationship was different now. She no longer seemed a protector, a confidant. Her magic diminished. I sensed her looking at us sideways most of the time.

In our new apartment, I studied my cookbooks like Ma studied hers. Listed ingredients for the week's groceries. Dad handed me a wad of cash and dropped me off at Star Market. I stood outside, leaning on a cart full of brown paper bags, waiting for his return. Every night I made a different meal for Dad, Michael, and me, just like Ma and Eleanor had done. On Saturday mornings, I cleaned bathrooms, washed everyone's laundry, vacuumed, and dusted, then spent afternoons at the barn with Dad's horses.

One evening, the phone rang.

"Hi Mary. This is Wallace. Kathy gave me your number."

My heart jumped out of hibernation.

He'd heard I moved. Wanted to see how I was. I explained about moving, the old house, the renovations. He promised to call back when he could borrow his mother's car.

At the barn, I hooked a leadline to Bonnie's bridle. Inside the corral, I held the lead out, clicked my tongue, and she trotted in circles. I stood in the center clicking and she continued trotting.

"Whoa," I said. She stopped. I approached her. Told her what a good girl she was. "You're next, big boy," I said to Louie as I walked over, placed the lead on him. He trotted around, something he'd remembered how to do like a human never forgets how to ride a bike. As the sun set and air cooled, I gave them a good brushing, then fed and watered them, before heading home to make dinner.

Another day I walked from behind the garage, stuck a bucket under the spigot, gave the handle a big turn, then stooped over it, waiting for the pail to fill up. As water pounded the bucket bottom, a shadow approached from behind. I turned, glanced up.

"Hi Mary Gayle," Eleanor said.

Dread. Sadness. Shame. Each emotion took his turn pulsating between my throat and head.

"You must like it over here where you have horses."

Was that sarcasm I sensed or was I imagining it?

"Hi," I said, turning the spigot off.

"Your father told me he fixed up the house as a nice new home for you all," she said. "I hope you're happy here. Aren't you going to ask me how Jeffrey is?"

"How's Jeffrey?" I said.

"He misses you and your father very much," she said.

Dad strolled over, looking as if caught alone in the kitchen at midnight with a fork in a whole chocolate cake.

Eleanor turned to Dad. "I was just saying you and Mary Gayle must be happy in your new place," she said.

"Well, why don't you come ova and see it?" he said.

My heart pounded.

"I'd like that," she said.

"Okay, lem-mee wash my hands," he said. "Mary Gayle, wanna ride ova with us?

"No, I can walk," I said. "I'll meet you there."

I rushed home, anticipating their arrival. They came a few minutes later and sat in the living room side by side on the voluptuous gold sofa.

I acted busy in the kitchen while listening to their conversation.

"It's nice," Eleanor said. "But it's not my taste."

"Do you wanna move in here with us?" asked Dad.

My chest tightened.

"No, it's not my taste," she said again. "Plus, I can't make my boys give up their rooms and come all the way over here. It wouldn't be fair."

I breathed. Walked into the living room.

"Would you like something to drink, Eleanor?" I asked, remembering she'd taught me to say, "Would you like...?" instead of "Do you want...?"

"What's the matter, you're not calling me, *Mom*, anymore, Mary Gayle?" she asked.

No words surfaced to articulate a response, so I said nothing. The truth was, I was overspent in our relationship. Dad had signed me up for this woman to become my new mother without my fully knowing her—or knowing *her and Dad* as a couple. I no longer could see how our bonds fit together. Calling her *Eleanor* again instead of *Mom* was the only way my young mind knew how to divest myself of that contract.

Chapter 8

Dad and Eleanor started seeing a lot of each other again. At first Dad stayed at her house just a few times a week. Then he moved back into her place. This time, he didn't ask me to come back with him. He just left us there—Michael and me as teens living upstairs in our own apartment with Dorothea, Bob, Donnie, and Todd in their apartment below us.

While Dad and Eleanor somehow achieved living together again, she and I managed tearing our relationship apart. Moving in. Moving out. Pain over Dad's exits. Bitterness in his casting me off on her. My flippant behavior. The rants. Running away. Weekend hours alone in my room. A shiny silver beer can.

One by one, these events, emotions, and behaviors ripped out the threads we'd sewn, manufacturing a mother–daughter relationship. A fragile relationship. Shopping. Baking peanut butter crisscross cookies. Discussing Ma's death and Eleanor's polio. Preparing Thanksgiving turkeys and Easter hams. Sniffing lemon balm, oregano, and basil at the Garrison House garden. Speech lessons. We hadn't finished the work. Her remaining stitches ripped out the day she found the beer can in my room. Mine when she dropped me off after the wild ride to Dad's.

I still saw Dad at his garage, though. Next time I got him to take me shopping for tack, I bought some Murphy's Oil Soap and a leather bridle and bit. Back at the barn, I placed Bonnie's new bridle on, wiggling the bit into her mouth. As calm as an angel, she walked around the corral on her lead. I told her, "Stand." She did. I hoisted myself onto her bare back. Patted her, tugged a rein to one side, and used my heel to nudge her. "Walk." Again, she walked around the corral. Dad, standing by his garage back door, stared my way, like a living statue. I rode Bonnie inside the corral that day, just walking, for about thirty minutes.

I gave the reins a gentle tug, signaling her to stop. She did. I leaned forward onto my belly, while lifting a leg around her backside and sliding down until my feet touched ground. "Good girl, Bonnie," I said while patting her for a moment. Then I groomed and fed her and Louie before walking home to make dinner.

A few weeks later, Dad bought me a western saddle. I began riding Bonnie outside the corral just a couple of miles at first—around our block. On one of my rides, I discovered a trail running past Dad's junk cars, through a narrow path along the back edge of Saint Joseph's Cemetery where Ma lays buried, into an open field, and toward a bridge and stream running under it—just like in my wallpaper. We approached the bridge. Bonnie pulled away. I hopped off and walked her over to it, letting her sniff the bridge, thinking she might walk over it if I led her. She pulled away. I hoisted myself back up onto her and returned to the barn, feeling a bit disappointed we couldn't get to the fields on the other side of that bridge.

The next several times I rode, we'd come back to that bridge. I'd slide down and try to lead her over.

"C'mon, girl. It's okay."

She'd pull away. I'd hoist myself back up onto her and return to the barn, feeling the same regret. Then one day, we approached the bridge, I got off, and as always, nudged her reins as I stepped onto it.

"C'mon, girl. You can do it."

To my delight, she walked right over the bridge without hesitation. Next time, and countless times to follow, I rode her over that bridge and into grassy hills and fields on the other side. I rode back out to the road on the far end, finishing miles from where we first entered the trail. Bonnie taught me a lesson that day that took years to absorb—accomplishments happen in stages. It takes patience. But crossing our bridges is so worth it because in doing so, we get to see what's on the other side.

Though it's a wonder I had the wherewithal to get a horse over a bridge. During my high school years, I was the kid who "fell through the cracks." Getting by on fair grades, heading in no good direction. Smoking weed in the woods beside our school most mornings with "freaks," as we were called. Freaks wore ripped jeans before they were fashionable. Freaks weren't interested in school events or sports or college. If they were boys, they kept their hair long—when being a hippie had gone out of style. If they were girls, they had a *reputation*. I didn't have a plan. Didn't know how to make one or where to find one.

I wish I had reached out to teachers and counselors who could have helped. I didn't hold the confidence, the sense of self-worth to walk into their offices and ask. They seemed unreachable to me. As if they wouldn't take me seriously. I considered myself incorrigible to them. Envying beautiful clothes other girls wore, I played proud in my holey jeans and worn hiking boots.

Losing Ma, I eventually lost myself, too. Beyond the departed person, loss is all that happens and doesn't happen in the void. As a child, I didn't know any kids my age who had lost mothers. Observing other girls with their moms over the years, at Girl Scout events, field trips, and carpools, for instance, left a sense whispering to my core that I was odd. An outcast. It felt lonely between those cracks.

Loss comprised all the rage I'd witnessed. It stepped along a tightrope of friction in relationships and broken bonds—and exhaustion from coping and *acting* normal. Loss embodied everything I missed hearing, thinking, and doing while daydreaming through noise and dysfunction. It comprised all I got away with. Loss haunted what might have been. It robbed what was supposed to be. It neglected my clothes and my hair and what I ate and how much I slept. A sense, and only a sense because I wasn't mature enough to analyze all this, that everyone else seemed better off. Loss delivered unworthiness.

I had a lot to be thankful for though, too. Didn't appreciate it then. I didn't know how to help myself. But I somehow knew how to help a horse over a bridge.

Many years after becoming a mother myself, it didn't take me long to embrace the loss anew—to realize just exactly what it was I had lost: an enormous and stubborn love. Love enough to fuel vigilance and guidance. Someone programmed to do what's best for a child—every waking minute of every single day for a lifetime.

Late fall about 1977, Wallace called saying he got wheels. He stood on our back porch. I invited him up. We talked as if we had seen each other every day without a blip. Next, we were making out on Dad's voluptuous sofa, then in darkness on my bed. The whole time I could hear loud *whrrrrrs* of some power tool Dad used next door at the garage.

"Have you ever, you know?" he whispered. "No, I haven't ever 'you know,'" I said.

He laughed, kissed my ear.

"Do you want to?" he said.

"Yes," I said, even though I wasn't sure I wanted to.

Claaang, went Dad's wrench or whatever metal object he just dropped. *No, maybe it's a crowbar. Whrrrr*, went his power tool, again.

Wallace unzipped his jeans and slipped them off. I had always helped fold laundry, witnessing myriad of men's underwear sizes coming out of our dryers. I thought it weird he had no underwear. Then he unzipped my pants and pulled them off. We left our shirts on.

He crawled on top of me and kissed me. *Vrooom, vroooom, vroom. Dad must be testing an engine.*

I felt nothing. Not passion. Not lust. It just felt uncomfortable. I wanted it over. My ears followed the *whrrrrrs* and *clangs* coming from the garage, straining for the engine of Dad's truck or the back door creaking open or footsteps thumping upstairs.

"Now you're a woman," he said.

"Thank you," was all I could think of. I didn't feel like a woman, and I wasn't thankful. I felt ashamed, disgusted. I wanted him to leave. We got dressed, said our goodbyes. As his mother's car rolled down the driveway, a gust of relief swept over me.

That year, I met a new friend in the designated smoking area, a spot by the dumpster just outside our high school cafeteria door. Alice had just moved from Seattle because her dad's job at Boeing relocated to Burlington, Massachusetts. Alice held her cigarette at the corner of her mouth and as she took it out, blew smoke from that same side.

People from elsewhere fascinated me. That same year, still about 1977, at school I befriended a Vietnamese refugee girl and a German boy from West Germany—while a wall still stood between East and West Berlin. The Vietnamese girl lived somewhere in town with her family. The German boy was an exchange student. None of us broke cultural barriers enough for becoming confidants. They seemed too well mannered.

Alice and I found a lot to talk about. At a time before internet and Facebook, people from states more than a day's drive away seemed exotic. I wanted to know about life out there, and she needed a friend here.

Alice oscillated between intellectual and party girl. Her mother took us to the Museum of Fine Arts in Boston—my first experience at an art museum—to see Beatrix Potter's watercolors. I envied Alice's doting over drawings of tiny bunnies, kittens, and mice. I learned to appreciate art by watching her that day.

Alice had her license. I didn't. When we went out, just about every weekend, Alice drove. One night before going out, she came over and fetched some pot and a pipe from her pocketbook.

"Wanna smoke a bowl," she said, smiling.

We went into my bedroom, sat on my bed. She lit up the bowl, took a long hit, and passed it to me. I took a hit and passed it back. We continued passing the pipe back and forth until we were sufficiently giggly. We tapped the ashes out in an ashtray, left the pipe on my nightstand, and headed for the movies.

Later that night, she dropped me off. The high had worn off. As I opened my back door, the inside door leading to Dorothea's apartment flew open. Dorothea stood there in rage—angrier than she was over the broken pumpkin.

"I found *this* in your room," she said, brandishing the pipe like a knife in my face. "What do you think you're doing?"

"Do you want to turn out like Jackie, a junkie?" she shrieked. "Is that what you want? What if Dad finds out? Did you ever think about that? And Eleanor. She would just love seeing you fall apart over here— and they would blame me! You are not getting this back, and if I ever catch you doing this again, so help me God, Mary Gayle, I will kill you myself with my bare hands."

She slammed her apartment door in my face.

I climbed upstairs toward my room, her screams still ringing in my ears. My knees shaking in my jeans and wobbling from fear. Back in my room, I noticed she had also confiscated my ashtray, matches, and little pot baggies. I don't remember how long it took me to fall asleep that night. I do recall it became some good many years before I ever smoked pot again—and never again under the same roof as my sister.

Wallace continued calling and visiting me. At one point, his mother took back her car. Sometimes he hired a cab to come see me. This seemed strange because living in suburbs, we didn't often see cabs in our neighborhood.

"Doesn't he have a job?" Dorothea asked.

"No, but I think he's looking," I said.

"Don't you think it's a little strange he's not working?" she asked. She left me with that thought.

Next time he came, he brought a large hiking backpack and asked if he could store it at our apartment. It swelled to the brim with his clothes and other personal articles. He said he needed a place for it. That he trusted me with it. Then he asked if he could stay that night and the next and the next and the next. Each time, I let him stay, fearing getting found out and shushing his every move. Once I left for school, he placed my dresser against my bedroom door, so no one could enter my room.

Jackie reappeared. Still on his clean streak. It was a Saturday afternoon. He knocked on my bedroom door.

"Mary Gayle, I need to speak to you," he said.

Wallace tiptoed over and stood against the wall, so he'd be behind that same door when it opened. I opened it. To my surprise, Jackie entered and sat on my bed. I sat beside him. We faced the open door Wallace was standing behind. I couldn't believe Jackie didn't know Wallace hid there.

"Mary Gayle, where's that Wallace guy?" he asked.

"I don't know," I said. "He's not here today."

"What is his goddamned backpack doing in your room?" he asked.

"He just left it here until he can find a place for it," I explained.

"He's a no-good, sleazy loser," said Jackie, raising his voice. "He has no place comin' around here and tryin'-a move in."

I studied my wallpaper's trees and bridges and streams running under them, wishing I could escape into my serene place with Bonnie.

"If I catch him in this bed, I will strangle him until his goddamned head pops off," Jackie said. "Do you understand?"

"Yes," I said.

He got up and walked out. My ears followed his hefty footsteps thudding downstairs toward Dorothea's apartment. After he closed the door at the bottom behind him, Wallace scurried from behind my bedroom door and began packing up all his loose belongings. He announced that as soon as everyone downstairs was in bed that night, he'd better go. He called a friend for a ride and slipped out into darkness. As their car engine faded, I felt a sense of relief. It took me that second sense of relief over this guy leaving to get it—that if you feel relieved over someone's departure, it's probably not a good idea to invite him back.

In his book, *The Noonday Demon*, Andrew Solomon writes, "Saint Anthony in the desert [when] asked how he could differentiate between angels who come to him humble and devils who come in rich disguise, said you could tell by the way you felt when they had departed. When an angel left you, you felt strengthened by his presence; when a devil left, you felt horror."

For years, decades, afterward, I felt so horrible about what I did with Wallace in my father's house that I couldn't even say his name to myself. Thinking about him made me wince. As I consider now the sex and the pot, I am so thankful for my older siblings. While I didn't have a parent's love in that house for the guidance I needed, love lived in that house. My siblings tried their best to keep me in line, to save me from myself. Even Jackie, carrying all his own demons, found a way to lift me out of the hellhole I'd begun digging for myself. My siblings pulled me out of the cracks and over the bridge. Though, I still had the hills to hike.

Chapter 9

The years leading up to my marriage seem more difficult to recall than my adolescence. Replaying this part of memory's reel-to-reel, scenes spilled off frames, some colorful, some, black and white. An occasional rip in the film, blurred images, and entire chunks of time missing. My graduation ceremony on Chelmsford High School's football field in springtime 1978. Dad, Eleanor, Dorothea, Bob, Donnie, and Michael, all there for me, again as they had been on my confirmation day—like one big happy family.

That summer, I said goodbye to Alice as she went off to college in California and to Kathy who packed up and headed for the Hartford Conservatory of Dance in Connecticut. I desired to go off somewhere, too. However, I hadn't done a thing to prepare. No SATs. Hadn't visited any colleges. Didn't complete admissions paperwork. Hadn't taken any other steps the school guidance counselors recommended and reminded and reminded and reminded us students to do.

Instead, I drove a few miles down the road and completed an application for work at a local cup factory, Comet Products. My job involved standing before a conveyor belt and dropping clear plastic cups adorned with brand logos—mostly hotels—one at a time, between two black dots, about five inches apart, marked on shrink wrap that sped on the belt. Further down the line, robotic arms descended upon those black lines and wrapped the cups individually in plastic. Wrapped cups then dropped off a cliff, through a chute, and into a pit where several women stood at the bottom, grabbing them, two hands at a time, and packing them into boxes. Speaking to co-workers required yelling over the machines' engines.

Whenever I dropped a cup *on*—instead of *between*—the dots, the robotic arm descended upon and squashed the cup, jamming the machine. This required the mechanic with long straight black hair to come and clear the jam. This happened often. Comet fired me within two months.

About a week later, I got an assembly job at Silicone Transistor, a small electronics company, still a few miles from home, where I daydreamed all day long for the next three years, using tweezers to place minute squares into tiny trays and attaching little metal wires to them. I continued living in the apartment above Dorothea and began paying Dad one hundred dollars a month for rent. I purchased my own food and clothes. Dad remained living at Eleanor's.

At home one night, Michael, at about twenty, became upset because his girlfriend threatened to break up with him. She cried. He ran from his bedroom holding a leather belt around his neck, pulling its long strap through the buckle, creating a noose. He held the long end above his head, threatening to hang himself.

Dorothea wasn't home, so I called Andy who lived around the corner.

Andy, wearing his blue work uniform, flew through the door and up the stairs, glared at Michael and yelled, "Stop this shit, right now. Do you understand, Michael? If I ever catch you doing this again, I'll knock the livin' daylights outta ya."

Then without another word, Andy stomped down the stairs and out the door, slamming it shut, our walls quaking behind him. Michael slowly removed the belt from his neck and slunk back into his room with the girl. They still broke up, and Michael never threatened to kill himself again.

This act, straight from Ma's suicide playbook, remained the single time Michael, in any way, expressed to me what he'd witnessed as a child all those years ago. No anecdote. No narrative. No explanation. Just an act, demonstrating he knew how to get the job done.

Michael also knew, as well as I did, precisely what Andy meant by his laconic reaction, devoid of all sympathy. *That there was no fucking way in hell we were all going through that again.* Andy had deployed one absolute directive with such explosive economy, it hauled Michael out of his dark head space to the reality only they two shared, shutting the whole episode down.

Soon afterward Jackie moved into our house's only third floor room. Things like jewelry and money went missing. My senior high school ring disappeared. A tax return check I depended on to pay my car insurance never came. I called the Internal Revenue Service. They said it was cashed more than a month ago, signed by me and a "John J. Ferreira." Cashed at Hore's Fish Market in Lowell, the city abutting Chelmsford. The shop owner believed Jackie when he said he was my husband.

Next morning, I marched over to see Dad at his garage and reported the stealing. I explained I didn't feel safe having Jackie in the house with Michael and me.

"I'll take care of it," he said.

Months went by. Nothing changed. I started a second part-time job as a cocktail waitress at Joseph's Lounge in Chelmsford. Joseph's seemed a classy place, featured talented bands, and attracted a professional crowd. As a waitress there, I wore black cocktail dresses. Weeks later, I packed my stuff and moved out and into an apartment in Lowell that I shared with a girl, a co-worker from Silicone Transistor.

Scenes from that era appear hazy. Got drunk, got stoned, and got laid by a young man-boy—after all, he was only about twenty-three—I met at Joseph's. At first, I tried considering him a boyfriend, even though he showed up only at two o'clock in the morning, the end of my shift, and left me by five am. Daydreaming through my first job and partying through my second one, I served as human plankton, traveling on everyone else's terms, allowing friends and employees to consume me as they wished.

There's a scene in the wonderful children's book *The Phantom Tollbooth*, by Norton Juster, where the protagonist Milo's toy car is stuck—won't budge. The watchdog in the story says to Milo, "Since you got here by not thinking, it seems reasonable to expect that in order to get out, you must start thinking." Juster eloquently details how with that, Milo begins thinking as hard as he can and "the wheels began to turn."

Betty, one of my former co-workers from Silicone Transistor, came back for a visit after leaving months earlier for a position at a large health insurance company. She mentioned I would probably like working there. Said they were hiring and handed me a paper with a name and phone number. After a brief interview process, I got the job at Aetna. My boss at Silicone, Marian, said she knew they would hire me because "you are very well spoken." I thought about my language lessons with Eleanor.

I started by attending the company training program—twelve weeks of classroom instruction. For months, I studied the human anatomy, medical terms and medical codes, and the intricacies of health insurance. On the job, I reviewed stacks of medical bills, operative reports, and prescription drug receipts, fascinated by all that people swallowed, had injected into, and excised out of their bodies. I matched each detail to those three- and five-digit codes and figured out their allotted payouts based on a complex taxonomy of rules-based formulas, customized by individual health plan design.

An incision or poke into the body (even splinter removal) was considered surgery. And surgery was paid at one hundred percent of the cost, unless it was for a non-covered procedure like a tubal ligation or vasectomy. Those were considered optional back then and not covered unless specifically stated in the plan or if coverage was required for such services under state law. And state law could mean the state in which the plan contract was written or where the claimant lived or where the surgery took place. Each type of service or supply such as office visits, lab work, prescription drugs, and medical equipment, etcetera, had its own set of Rube Goldberg rules.

To keep my head clear enough to concentrate, I stopped partying. Moved into a quieter studio apartment on the other side of town and lived there alone. I got by on two jobs. While it wasn't apparent then, I was investing in skills that would generate dividends in future years.

On weekends at about twenty, the legal drinking age in Massachusetts at that time, I still went out, but with a tamer crowd of girls. A popular local spot in Lowell, The Raft, featured folk guitarists upstairs and a dance floor with a DJ playing new wave downstairs. I hung downstairs. I grew so comfortable at The Raft, it felt like walking into my own living room on a Saturday night with friends.

In September 1981, a young guy sitting at the bar smiled at me and asked if I'd like to buy him a drink. Maybe because he looked like Mick Jagger. Maybe his British accent. Perhaps a combination of these factors. Whatever the reasons, I ended up marrying Brian three years later.

My siblings and I all eventually made peace with Dad and Eleanor, visiting them at Eleanor's house during Christmastime and other holidays. She and Dad still warred, but at least we kids no longer took bullets in their crossfire. At twenty-three, I called her, reporting I was marrying Brian at month's end and planning a small affair. She became engrossed in every detail.

"Every daughter deserves a wedding," she said and convinced Dad to spring for a big one. "I want to buy your wedding gown."

She took me shopping for a gown. There, we had come full circle, with me in the dressing room and her peeking in from the corner of the curtain to see how my new dress fit.

On my wedding day, Eleanor strolled down the aisle to "Amazing Grace," playing her role as mother-of-the-bride. At the back of the church, I wondered if I was the wretch in the song being saved. Dorothea, in her satin maid-of-honor gown, looked, as always, as flawless as an angel. There was Dad, walking me down the aisle exuding pride on his face and in his stance. Like on my graduation day, we appeared "family-ish" as if normal—all of us patching up pain in swaths of white silk and lace.

As a family, we didn't talk much about Ma's death or even about Ma. We simply picked up and went on in silence without her. After carrying this silence through my childhood, I took it all the way to the altar. Carried it through two pregnancies and into early motherhood. Hauled it into and out of divorce court with me. Dragged it through single motherhood until I couldn't lug it around with me any longer.

Part 2

Eighteen Years Later

Chapter 10

Boom! Boom! Our upstairs bathroom walls quivered. It was August 2001. My marriage to Brian had just disintegrated. As a mother at about forty-one, I tried to create a new home with my two sons and our miniature poodle in a double-unit condo located in Uxbridge, a small town about an hour south of Chelmsford. The boys were eight and eleven. An impatient older couple lived on the other side of our walls.

A newer place providing no grates in its floors or alcoves to hide in, this house held nothing special for me. As I walked in, it seemed to say, "Who the hell are you and what are you doing here? Besides, I don't like that you took the duck border down in the kitchen and painted the walls yellow. Could you put that goddamned duck border back up, lady?"

Its only redeeming quality was that it sat way back off the road, hidden by trees. Hiding felt good because divorce felt raw. Early divorce carried the paranoia of a pothead, even though I was straight. The nakedness of a stripper, even when I was clothed. I became an outcast among friends and family. It felt best to stay back, lie low.

Ready for bed in pajamas, Geoff, my older son, just let the toilet cover drop to a slam, as he often did.

Boom! Boom! Boom!

"Mom, what was that?" Greg cried.

"Oh, they're probably moving furniture over there," I called from my bed across the hall.

Boom! Boom! Boom! More shaking. More vibrating.

"Mom, I think they're banging on the walls," Geoff said, water running from the facet.

"You know what? I think you're right," I said.

He came in for a goodnight hug.

"Maybe it's their way of telling us they want to sleep. Let's keep quiet," I said.

We never lived under the same roof as neighbors before. When my boys' baseballs landed in their pool, the husband scolded them. When their bikes skidded and scattered mulch like broken glass, he grumbled at them. At night, the older people on the other side banged the walls—signaling for us to pack it in. I think the wife was the wall banger. Besides when the toilet cover slammed, we heard her banging when we tossed balls to Midnight inside, laughed aloud, and it seemed, any time she could hear us. The wall banging made me feel more like a temporary boarder facing eviction than a homeowner.

Another neighbor mentioned that on the day before we moved in, she observed our realtor placing a plant on our doorstep, and also that she witnessed the wall-banging wife moving that plant to *her* doorstep.

Our home before divorce, located across town, stood big and proud. It was another newer place without a soul. On a quiet street where everyone had their own tidy yards, we hosted dinner guests, birthday parties, and holidays there. In our custom-built kitchen I set up a sundae buffet with homemade chocolate syrup, butterscotch, and fresh whipped cream. My then husband, Brian, monitored a variety of backyard games we'd rigged for our son's birthday—miniature golf, toss the bag, hoops.

One-by-one as parents picked up their children, they complimented us on our lovely home and creativity. We looked good on the outside, just like my family did when I was growing up.

The events and sentiments surrounding my marriage's demise—like most couples'—are complicated. It isn't fair for one individual to articulate all cracks and fissures triggering a divorce obviously happening between two individuals. It should suffice to say I hold as much blame for our breakup as he should. Brian never missed his Wednesday nights and every other weekends caring for our boys. Except for matters concerning them, we remained out of each other's life.

After moving into Wall Banger condo, I couldn't bring myself to invite people over—and I hated my own shameful pride in that. Last time I remembered feeling so jolted by life was the day Ma died.

Life alone with the boys and Midnight seemed strange and scary. With divorce, I lost several friends and my ex-husband's entire family. I lost a beaded-edge, dark wooden dining room set, artwork from a coastal community dealer, dishes, a ride-on lawn mower. That big house. Most important, I lost the sacred bond of a family I tried making to have a whole one again. Caring for two kids and a miniature poodle, working, and getting an education—I juggled more alone than ever.

Taking on a pacifist's attitude toward our neighbors, I avoided war with them. If they banged their walls, I ignored them. When they grumbled, I apologized and tried to teach my boys about respecting the property.

While I would have loved to spend more hours caring for the boys as I had pre-divorce, I had to haul in an income. Up until Geoff was about three, I earned a series of promotions at that large health insurance company I worked for. Once Greg came along, I quit and become a stay-at-home mom. I retooled my skills, taking evening courses at a nearby college.

After divorce, a reporter position opened at a local paper, *The Blackstone Valley Tribune*. It seemed the perfect place to begin again. I covered everything from local politics, to arts and events. My colleagues and I worked from a storefront in downtown Whitinsville, a village in Northbridge, Massachusetts named after the behemoth Whitin mill building stretching a good length of Main Street. You can't drive through this old mill town without passing a church in every neighborhood.

A staff of three, we reporters covered a few local communities—small town fare. With only an associate's degree, I began classes toward the bachelor's degree from Clark University in Worcester I should have earned twenty years earlier instead of daydreaming away three years of my life at Silicone Transistor.

An early twenty-something, our editor was half my age. I can't recall her last name, but I'll never forget how her redlines made me feel about my writing—like bathing suits made me feel about my body. Until I got into the weeds of her markups.

"Please explain who John Kerry is," she scrawled in red ink across my copy. "If I don't know who it is, someone else might not know it."

"You don't know it because you are ignorant," I thought. Then I incorporated her revision.

Our only other writer, Tom, was a decades-long newspaper man. A Harvard grad in his sixties, he talked as if he had a bent coat hanger in his mouth. His talent was exponentially greater than the job required. He strung and seasoned his words and judged himself or his readers on the comments they made about his stories. If Tom got negative feedback or none at all, he'd often say, "Mediocre only knows itself."

Holding one eyebrow raised, pointing at my redlines from the editor, he said, "Just remember, if she couldn't do that to your work, she wouldn't have a job." Then he'd smile and give a reassuring nod. Tom offered to review my work first whenever we had time. He identified grammar lessons I slept through in Mrs. Brown's fifth-grade English class. Tom provided remediation to make my verbs parallel, avoid misplaced modifiers, and punctuate where it mattered.

"You never really must say, 'In order to…' just get rid of the words 'in order.' It will sound cleaner… Start your sentences with a verb—they'll come alive. Don't be afraid to ask them to repeat their quotes so you can get every word just as they say it."

The paper paid below the federal poverty level, but my reporting, parenting, and night classes wrapped nicely around each other. I could get my kids off to school, run to the office, get back home for dinner, and cover municipal events at night. Classes and homework fit in between.

As a single mom juggling family, work, school, housework, a dog, and all the rest, I felt like an engine always on at full throttle. I couldn't get it all done and never made it on time for anything. Early mornings. Late nights. Fell asleep within moments of getting into bed and jumped up as soon as my alarm clock screeched. Following long days at work, I cooked—American chop suey, macaroni and cheese, and chicken parmesan. Sometimes I made crockpot dinners—until Geoff said they all tasted the same, even if ingredients were different. I wanted to be like Ma that way.

Occasionally for breakfast, I fried Popeye eggs for my boys like she did. Except mine were made with whole grain rather than Wonder Bread and a heart-shaped hole in the center rather than a rough circle carved with a butter knife. And I didn't smoke a Winchester while cooking—or at any other time as a mother.

"Mom, why are they called Popeye eggs?" Geoff asked.

"I don't know. That's just what my mother called them," I said.

"How did your mother die, Mom?" Geoff asked.

"She was very sick," I said.

"What kind of sickness did she have?" he asked.

"She was just very sick, but don't worry, I don't have that kind of sickness. It's not hereditary."

His curiosity about Ma's death amazed me. Ma was *my mother* and I never asked *how* she died when I was a little girl.

As a single mother, leaving for my long workday often meant packing for a short stay away. I never organized my day enough to remember everything. However, I made and revised long to-do lists for my life. I read books like Napoleon Hill's *Think and Grow Rich*, which asserts thought is matter, the first chain in a string of events in making something happen. Besides my daily to-do lists, I maintained a long list of all actions I could possibly take, thoughts I could possibly think to move closer to a better life as Napoleon Hill advised. I printed this plan, pages and pages of it, and read it every night before bed, checking off actions accomplished, crossing off what no longer belonged, and adding new tasks. When my plan became a mass of handwritten scribbles, I typed in my changes and printed the revision, rendering my plan legible again.

Despite my hectic life and low pay, I became captivated by people and scenes from reporting, getting tossed into events and among types I'd never otherwise encounter. As employees, we took turns opening our office. One hot summer day, I stood outside our one-story brick building wiggling the key in the lock. Hearing the phone ringing inside only made the fussy key more frustrating. When the lock gave way, I burst in, running over the dirty rug, past the plastic plants in the lobby, down the ink-smudged pink hallway to my metal desk—that probably held a Smith Corona electric typewriter in its heyday.

"Tribune, Mary speaking."

It was Tim, our managing editor, saying the Douglas Forest was on fire and telling me to get there right away.

"And get a picture of helicopters dipping water out of the reservoir," he called as I started hanging up.

"Okay," I said, even though I didn't know what he meant about helicopters. I'd figure it out later. Running back toward my car, I realized I wouldn't have worn a dress that morning had I planned on traipsing through smoldering woods alongside firefighters. At the scene, though, it wasn't quite like that. A fireman instructed me to stay outside the forest at the fire department's staging area. Still, I spoke with guys resting between shifts. No one knew what started it. "Maybe a campfire" seemed their best guess. I chatted with a photographer from a larger paper, mentioning I needed a shot of some helicopters.

"Come on," he said.

"Where are we going?" I said, trotting after him.

"The reservoir," he said.

We jumped in his 1990s Buick. He sped through a causeway where helicopters were hovering low over water, causing massive ripples. He pulled over. Helicopter pilots dropped down buckets, scooped up water, slowly rose, and swooped over the fire to dump them. My photograph landed on our paper's cover. A fire one day, a court trial the next, a day at a school charity, or on some politician's campaign trail the next—I never knew what was coming until it came.

In December 2001, Dorothea called saying Dad fell in his garage and broke his hip. Over the years after Ma's death, Dad and I had grown apart. We stayed friendly. Always found him at his garage. But he never checked in on me and the boys. I had to make an effort to contact him. If I vanished, I wasn't so sure he'd hunt for me as he'd done years ago when I ran away as a troubled teen.

But he remained my dad, my only parent. That's why I didn't hesitate racing to Lahey Hospital in Burlington, about an hour from Whitinsville, to see him that day. My siblings sat in a waiting room. Dad and Eleanor had divorced many years earlier, and Eleanor had little contact with him as a result. The surgeon finally arrived, told us the fracture repair went well, and Dad should recover just fine.

Instead of getting better in the months following surgery, Dad suffered as his lungs filled with fluid. Complications of diabetes and heart disease exacerbated his condition. Rushing to Lahey as often as I could never seemed enough. Whenever I wasn't by Dad's bed, I carried a constant guilt about his lying helpless and fighting for his life. How could anything else be more important? I lugged the guilt in my chest and went about my business anyway.

I also carried the notion—maybe from my Catholic upbringing or maybe planted by Cinderella—that my home wouldn't be complete again until I had a man in it, and that I needed to find one. The problem with this expectation was I never learned to navigate the complexities of relationships. Whether due to my observations of Dad's venture into remarriage or my own immaturity, it didn't play out well for me. What's worse, I remained blind to my shortcomings relating to men. In fact, I thought I *needed* a husband.

That's why with Peter, Dennis, Bill and others, my mind went off-roading, away from a sense of family obligation, prudence, and frugality. I met them online, during an era when internet dating had just emerged as a path for finding your special someone. Friends in settled relationships, considered it a dangerous endeavor—warning that lunatics and perverts lured their victims online. My single friends knew better. They said finding Mr. Right online required playing a "numbers" game. That I must go on a plethora of horrible dates first.

After my divorce, I met my share. A man who on the first (and only) date described three graphic scenes from tragic deaths of childhood friends he witnessed losing as a teenager. A guy who asked on a second (and final) date if he could take out his penis and hold it while we talked in his car. A guy with whom I dined, picnicked, paddled, explored the city on warm breezy nights, and shared romance and heart-to-heart talks for an entire summer—before he mentioned, *in an email message,* he had a fiancée.

That last one left me heartsick even though I'd only known him a couple months. Delusional, I continued pursuing him even after he broke the news. I called several times. He didn't pick up. I wrote him emails. He ignored them. Weeks later, his name popped up in my inbox. I clicked it open. The ensuing shock caused the full contents of my intestines to loosen, sending me rushing to my bathroom. The note contained a nasty message from his fiancée demanding I stay away from her man.

That's what it took for me to leave him alone. It destroyed me. I cried for weeks every chance I got. I couldn't take loss or rejection. I was a child inhabiting a woman's body.

Sitting with Dad one night at the hospital, Michael and I were watching a popular television show at the time, *Fear Factor*. In the show, the host dared contestants to endure dangerous and grotesque feats. This time contestants sat before bowls of raw sheep brains, which they committed to eat.

"Augh," I said.

"Gross," Michael said.

"What, I ate that all the time as a kid," Dad said.

Michael and I cracked up. This became the last conversation I remember having with Dad. One of the rare occasions when he shared a tidbit about life during his childhood—when he and siblings survived poverty. Dad always thought as long as he saved his family from financial ruin, nothing else mattered.

Sometimes a month went by between my visits to see him at Lahey. During one such stretch, Dorothea called saying Dad's condition grew critical. He had slipped into a coma. I dropped everything and ran.

At Lahey, Dorothea, Bob, Andy, Michael, Jackie, and I took turns with Dad day and night. Tubes down his throat, up his nose, in his veins. Erratically and often, as if possessed by demons, his eyes widened, teeth clenched, body stiffened and shook. Lahey medical staff assured us Dad wasn't suffering during those seizures. That he was unaware.

Our siblings left. Michael sat by one side of Dad's bed, I on the other. Just after midnight, this poor man began coughing. A gray matter spewed from his mouth. We rushed for a nurse who hurried in and suggested we get ourselves coffees. That she'd clean him up while we were away. When we returned, Dad was gone. The nurse mentioned how Dad took his right hand and nobly placed it on his heart just before leaving us.

She left us alone with Dad. I made the sign of the cross over my father's body. Michael stood solemn. We stepped outside the room and took turns calling our siblings. We walked to the parking lot together, hugged, and said goodbye.

Dad was eighty-one when he died that April night in 2002. After witnessing his suffering, I felt relieved for his passing. Still, I sensed a new aloneness having both parents gone, like roots under me severed.

My siblings and I discussed memorial arrangements. Dorothea said Dolan Funeral Home had an antique hearse for transporting Dad's body to the church and cemetery. Not a creepy long-stretch black hearse, but a brown 1927 Velie Henney hearse. That car could have driven straight off a scene from *Downton Abby*. I knew Dad would have loved that. He savored his time working on antique cars. He'd once restored a 1920 Ford pick-up truck.

My siblings had more plans for seeing Dad off. Over his career, Dad helped many people get into towing businesses, so Michael gleamed while mentioning a tow truck procession—many guys whom Dad mentored planned to drive their tow trucks, lights flashing and all, behind the antique hearse on the ride to the cemetery. It seemed kitschy. I'd always been proud of Dad for starting and managing his own business. A technical genius, the man figured out how to hoist cars from all manner of ditches, diagnose their faulty engines before computers could do it for him, then fix those cars.

He'd often tried helping people stranded by breakdowns. Heck, one Thanksgiving, Dorothea made corpulent turkey sandwiches on fresh bulky rolls with cranberry sauce, lettuce, mayonnaise, and stuffing. She bagged them up with chips and pickles. Dad delivered this picnic to a family confined to a local hotel room due to car trouble while traveling to relatives for their feast that year.

But there remained something about the stereotypical tow truck guy that bothered me when people applied it to Dad. The idea of a tow truck procession screamed to the world we were crooks who'd steal someone's last dime when they were down on their luck. We were dirty. Uneducated *wildlings* who'd pilfer the carnage of a rolled over tractor trailer truck for its cargo if valuable and salvageable.

I've often sensed that in judging me, guys I've dated gave extra points based on what important men in my life—my father and ex-husband—did for a living. As if like an animal, I am highbred or lowbred based on who raised or chose me. I perceived our tow trucks conveyed lowbred. I lost points for that. These selfish thoughts smoldered in my head. Ugly thoughts. However, this was Dad's day, not mine, I told myself. I pulled into Dolan's parking lot and noticed about six tow trucks parked outside, all in a row.

After church services, I shared a ride with Brian and our boys. Dorothea and her family rode ahead of us. In front of her stretched those several tow trucks. Light, medium, and heavy duty. Together, the magnitude of their rotating amber strobe lights—mounted on the fronts, sides, backs, and tops of all those trucks—blazed like Times Square on a Tilt-A-Whirl. Leading the parade, the antique hearse crept toward Saint Joseph's Cemetery. There were scores of cars behind us as far as vision stretched.

As our spectacle inched toward the cemetery, people on the street stood and gawked. Some laughed. Some pointed. I crouched in the passenger's seat. We came upon Dad's garage on the way. Precisely in front of the building, the hearse stopped. I figured perhaps the funeral director wanted to give Dad one last moment with his special place. Or maybe the director decided to give mourners a chance to see the flowers and signs Michael set out that read, "We love you Dad! We'll Miss You!"

However, one minute turned into two, then five, then I don't know how many. I opened my door and stepped out to see what happened, as those in cars behind us began doing, too. The hearse's hood stood up. Tow truck drivers in their suits milled around it. Word made it to our car that the hearse broke down and couldn't be easily repaired. They'd have to tow it.

My nephew and Jackie's son, Chris, who was one of the drivers, pulled his ramp truck out of the procession. Swung the truck over to the hearse, backed up, and hoisted the hearse, with Dad's coffin *and him in it,* onto the bed. Chris got out and worked controls on his truck. He and other guys inspected and secured chains under the hearse. Chris jumped back into his truck and led the entire procession, an oscillating illumination in one grand finale toward Saint Joseph's.

Walking toward the cemetery chapel for final prayers, cousins and other relatives marveled over what they witnessed as a miracle.

"That's your dad's way of getting in one last prank," someone said.

I wasn't sure what to make of it, but there was no doubt this tow truck extravaganza couldn't have been more appropriate—and my lowbred tow truck family perception dissipated from my head for good.

Maybe because we'd grown distant or given that Dad lived a long life. It could have been because he no longer suffered or that I was an adult. Or that he'd died a more natural death than my mother. Whatever combination of reasons, I didn't feel as shocked and as broken as when we lost Ma.

Dad didn't have a lot of money. For a time he'd held land nearby, considering it sort of a nest egg. Then he sold it for a $90,000 alimony payout to Eleanor decades earlier. The only possessions he left were his house and a mortgage on his garage when he sold it to Michael. Without a will, his estate landed in probate court. By the time his affairs were settled, there was close to nothing left for me and my siblings. Suffice to say I would continue getting ahead only through my own efforts. No handouts.

It seemed a wonder that almost two weeks after losing Dad, I met Henry, a car guy. We sat at the restaurant bar of a historic inn in western Massachusetts. He was forty-nine. I was forty-two. His hair seemed grayer than that of other men I dated. His face appeared a bit gaunt, but his smile lit up my heart. Within a couple of glasses of cabernet, I imagined his playing catch with my boys in our backyard while I picked a bouquet of flowers from a nearby garden.

He loved anything that went *vroom*. Raced a yellow Porsche at local tracks for kicks. Toured Tibet by motorbike. Traveled several times a month all over the country, all over the world sometimes, for his job and for adventure. Devoured books on these trips. But seeing happy couples at bars and restaurants while away sometimes got to him. Henry loved Vermont, one of my favorite places because of Uncle Sonny and Auntie Jeannie. He'd ridden a horse to school one day as a teenager, which reminded me of my days riding Bonnie. His parents enjoyed retirement together. His mother baked homemade Greek cookies. He divorced a decade ago. Never had kids, but loved his nieces and nephews. He desired a woman with whom he could connect on multiple levels, not just physical.

We began spending every other weekend together—the boys' weekends at their dad's. In summer, we picked berries, went for motorbike rides, visited his family. Sailing in a hot air balloon where the wind wanted—above fields, hills, and ponds of Post Mills, Vermont— we soaked in our pilot's stories about sights below.

"There is a cow at that farm giving the greatest milk production in the country," the pilot said, pointing toward expansive green hilly fields and a red barn below.

"Is there a reason for this phenomenon, a special diet?" I asked.

"No. She's just a really big cow," he said, pulling his cord to descend a bit for a better view.

He pointed out a house where another farmer lived—whose wife gave him a gift certificate for a hot air balloon ride a decade ago.

"Farmer never cashed it in," our pilot said. "I even landed in his field one day, but he said he'd have to wait for fall."

Later in his car, Henry had me in stitches, impersonating the curmudgeon as he imagined him.

"Never get me up in that goddamned contraption," Henry said, crusting up his voice.

In fall, we picked apples and baked pies, freezing some for Thanksgiving. That holiday, I had the day off. My boys were spending it with Brian. I let their dad take them most Thanksgivings and Easters. On Christmases, I kept the boys for the morning. Brian took them for the next two days to his family festivities. Since Ma died, my family became increasingly more fragmented and didn't get together much. At least Brian had a father, stepmother, brother, and sister-in-law, nieces, and nephews who gathered on holidays.

Henry invited me to spend Thanksgiving with him and his family. His parents' table seated at least twenty people, spanning two rooms. His father, two brothers and their wives, a sister, her husband, nieces, nephews, cousins, cousins' girlfriends, and family friends all gathered around that table while his mother grabbed last-minute dishes from the oven before joining her family at the table, just like Ma did. This big friendly family strengthened the notion that I found the right one. I belonged. Sharing the pies we baked from apples we picked earlier that fall cemented the "us" we had become.

During wintertime, we cooked and watched movies. We talked about literature, art, and faraway places we dreamed of exploring—Africa for me and across the United States on motorbike for him. He would one day do both; I would do neither.

While driving down Route 91, a major Connecticut highway, he mentioned he wasn't bothering with a Christmas tree that year—2002.

"But you should put up a tree," I said. "It doesn't matter that you live alone. It will help you get into the holiday spirit."

At that second, in the middle of the passing lane, there laid a Christmas tree. He swerved into the breakdown lane.

"Wait, you're not going for that one, are you?" I said. "It must belong to some family who just lost it. They'll be back for it."

Without a word, he jumped out of his car.

"You could be killed," I screamed after him.

He ran into the road, paused a few seconds, avoiding speeding cars, then ran up and grabbed it. He dragged the tree toward his Audi and hoisted it onto his car top. He jumped back in and opened the sunroof. We reached overhead and clasped the prickly trunk, holding on until we got to his place, hands freezing, cracking up the entire way.

I had mixed feelings about leaving him on late Sunday afternoons. I wanted to stay but cherished Sunday night dinners with my boys. I always tried to have something good bubbling on our stove as they walked in. At one Sunday night dinner, Geoff got curious about my life during their weekends with Brian.

"Mom, what do you do when we go to Dad's?" he asked between bites of pasta.

"Oh, just work or do chores here. Not too much," I said, sparing him distraction of my private life.

As much as I loved time with Henry, I dreamed of a different life. One like Ma's without everything going wrong. That of a mother who tended to her children and home and a husband who returned to her bed every evening. But reality spoke its truth. I witnessed what unhappiness can do to a woman over time. A breaking point awaits—maybe for all of us. I wouldn't allow myself anywhere near its edges—or so I thought.

At work, my reporting and writing skills were improving. I never knew the true essence of a story until I got into it. At the *Tribune* one day, I expected to run downtown to cover demolition of a paper company building. At the scene, a bulldozer crawled over to the structure, bit chunks out of it and exposed its interior, like a dollhouse. All these people stood watching, wearing pensive faces, some tearing up. After talking with them, I went back and wrote, not about demolition, but about that building's history. It served as Whitinsville's first funeral home, carried to town in the minds of returning World War II soldiers who shared stories of European families laying out their deceased loved ones in such places, rather than in living rooms.

I'd recount my day's reporting to Henry later—testimony I heard at court about two Rottweilers that dragged a child from her mother's arms and released her only after a local carpenter slammed a hammer into the dogs' heads. Elderly ladies who decorated floats at California Rose Bowl parades each year. Politicians, parents, law enforcement people, judges, local business owners, librarians, and others who shared their stories and their beefs. No matter how humble, intelligent, arrogant, or simple, everyone told a story worth hearing. To fill leftover space, I wrote a weekly garden column called *The Pruned Print*. Had a goal of climbing to a larger publication after a couple of years. But that wouldn't be.

I still earned fast-food-chain pay at the paper and received Walmart-cashier pay for child support. I managed getting by on my own from age seventeen when I graduated from high school and started paying Dad rent. Post-divorce became a first for trying it while caring for two kids. I knew better than letting the mortgage go, but the other necessities—food and Vans shoes Geoff wanted for skateboarding and Adidas cleats Greg requested for baseball and soccer—put my finances over the edge. As did manicures, clothes, and haircuts, powered by my desire for love and romance, and one day, a man in my home again. When I started digging out credit cards to pay for groceries and clothes and gas, I knew I needed to earn more.

That's why my plan to ratchet up a journalism career ladder wasn't to be. *Milford Daily News*, a larger local paper, hired me for a pittance more than the *Tribune* paid. However, a week before my first day, I got an offer for a corporate communications copywriter position at a large health insurer. They liked my combination of health insurance and writing experience and offered twice as much as *Milford Daily* paid, plus free health coverage. Responsible for kids and a mortgage, a clear path appeared before me. I sacrificed my stepping-stone toward an even bigger publication. Fighting the wrench in my gut, I bought a couple of suits and returned to corporate America.

In joining my new department, it seemed I walked in late for a party. As if guests and their host—all women—sat there sipping their cocktails and getting giddy with each other for hours before my arrival. Hadn't anyone expected me to attend this soirée, too? That I'd also been invited?

A senior writer who reviewed my work seemed most appalled by my presence. "Avoid starting sentences with a verb," she scolded. "Say 'in order to' instead of just 'to.' Don't use quotes of our senior executives exactly as they say them. Here, writers *craft* quotes and attribute them to our subjects."

Just as my old newspaper colleague, Tom, did, she could raise just one eyebrow at a time, too. When he made this gesture, he conveyed, "You know what I mean?" When she did it, she seemed to say, "What the hell's wrong with you?"

I cowered. Trying to make the best of my job, I pulled words together for health insurance handbooks, physician newsletters, internal news and announcements, ads, and patient health literature. I had to bend my writing and behavior toward *corporate-ese*. In a corporate office, cushioned from the external world of our customers, we "scripted" everything—as if writing a screenplay where our customers suffered, and we saved them. In the newsroom, we served on front lines of reality. Our customers and our readers *were* our stories, rather than a distant aberration of the people we were supposedly serving. Corporate communications were *crafted*. News stories were real.

Walking out to the parking lot after work one evening, I ran into my boss, one of the women from the "cocktail party." I mentioned heading to class.

"Oh, that's right. I'd heard you had some catching up to do," she said.

Her words hit me in the gut. I turned my key in the ignition. Up to that point, I thought I was "getting ahead," not "catching up." What a loser I was.

Scheduling extra office hours with my English professor, I absorbed this older woman's guidance and pointers on improving my corporate writing. Then I got home late at night and found a handwritten envelope in my mailbox from Henry. He wrote actual notes and dropped them in actual mailboxes. I placed a pot on to boil and made tea just right before opening it. A small celebration to end another painful day. I tore at the envelope carefully to avoid damaging it as much as possible. I slipped a card out. Flowers on the cover. Inside a blank card on which he wrote a note.

"The lightning is flashing. Thunder booming and rolling down..."

At work, my skills eventually developed enough for a promotion to senior writer. I earned my rite of passage into the tribe. Still, compared to what I'd done as a journalist, my work felt biased and superficial.

By then, Henry and I had been seeing each other for more than a year. Despite a sense of foreboding about his meeting my kids, I thought we should start "blending," that he should spend time not just with me, but with me and my boys.

One day I introduced him to them. Greg averted eye contact. Geoff acted nonchalant. Next time Henry came to see us, we all went out to dinner at a Mexican restaurant. My boys jumped and jostled their ways into his back seat.

"I want that side," said one.

"No, I'm getting it," said the other.

Henry turned around and irritably mocked them, "Nahhh, Nah, nah, nah. Nahh."

I was stunned. My perfect love was capable of being nasty. My boys fell silent. In fact, we all stayed quiet for the remaining car ride. Sitting in front of nachos and guac, he seemed miserable. I *Pollyanna-ed* my way through dinner to compensate for his ill demeanor. I couldn't wait to get home with my boys and for him to leave us.

Next time I saw him, I came alone.

"Can I just see you alone from now on," he asked.

"I guess so," I said.

His umbrella of affection for me didn't open wide enough for my kids to squeeze under, too. I figured I just wasn't loveable enough for a man to extend his affection beyond me to my children. I wasn't worthy of that level of devotion.

Was this the thinking of a motherless daughter? As humans, we suffer so many calamities over the years, it's impossible to discern which ones break us down and build us up. Carrying this mindset, I continued seeing Henry every other weekend. Months later, we went to Manhattan for a weekend. Our Saturday morning began peering through magnifying glasses, examining details of eyes and flower petals in da Vinci drawings at the Museum of Modern Art. We shared an afternoon of drinks and conversation in a swanky little SoHo pub. I can't recall the name. I only remember our small wooden table amid a brick-walled room. Crowds of people—beautiful people—walking by to the bar, back from the bar. Talking. Laughing. Just white noise of our bliss. We clinked glasses—his Bloody Mary. My cabernet.

"So how are you doing?" he asked.

"It gets hard sometimes," I said. "You know, juggling school and work and all."

"Do you want to move in with me?" he said, studying the plastic skewer he swirled in his drink.

"What about my kids?" I asked.

No answer.

He could be the man of my dreams only if my boys were not in our fantasy. The sentiment created static between us. Still months later, we were away another weekend for my birthday at an elegant inn near the Connecticut shoreline, about three hours from my home. We settled into our luxurious room. A king bed waited for us. A heated marble bathroom floor warmed my feet while I freshened my lipstick and eyeliner. We went to dinner at a nearby restaurant, with tickets in his pocket for an opera next door afterwards. The waitress filled our water glasses and took drink orders, later dinner orders.

As we finished eating, he said, "I have dated other women who had kids and it was fine. I don't know what it is about your kids. I just don't feel comfortable around them."

Set off by some primal instinct, I had an immediate need to get away from him.

"I need to use the restroom," I said. "I'll be right back."

After I returned, he paid the check. We walked over to the opera house. Climbing steps toward marble pillars, that same "fight or flight" instinct took hold of my mind again, this time stronger. I stopped and glared at him.

"I can't go in there with you," I said.

"What?" he said.

"I can't go in there with you," I repeated. "I want to go home."

"You're kidding," he said.

"No, I need you to take me home right now," I said.

"Okay," he said and pursed his lips.

In his Audi, I cried and again demanded—now screaming—to "go home."

He drove and sighed. I whimpered. For three hours.

Then he dropped me off.

Chapter 11

Henry and I tried talking and finding some common ground for moving forward, but the incident left us broken. He started finding reasons to stay away on weekends or vacation without me. Finally, he asked to see me at my condo one evening after school. My kids were at Brian's. I rushed home on hope. As I entered, the whiff of roasted chicken he cooked in my kitchen conveyed we were all right. His shaky laughter and regretful sighs at dinner said otherwise. On the sofa in my living room afterward, I gazed at him. The forever in his eyes had gone.

"I don't love you," he confessed. "I don't think I ever did."

Just as my aunties couldn't soothe my desperation the day Ma died, he couldn't comfort me against the barrage of questions I shot at him. "Are you seeing someone else? How could you say you loved me before if you didn't? How could you lead me on like that? Why didn't you tell me before? Can't we try a little harder?"

So again, I disintegrated into a heap of sobbing. He held me for a little while. Then he got up, walked over to the sliding glass door, and slipped out into night.

It felt as if I just tripped and fell hard during a fast run. As if my questions were begging him to break my fall. I went down. He couldn't do anything to stop it. I hit bottom. As pain lit up my chest, my mind raced to assess which parts of myself were broken.

During the following days, the loss of Henry, of my reporter job, and of my marriage marched into my chest and met the slow simmering grief from Ma's death. Each hurt carried its own torch and together, ignited a white-hot pain. I was worthless. A mess. Nobody owned me. I had catching up to do. I walked, talked, ate, slept, worked, and even fake-laughed carrying a pain I never thought possible to endure.

The truth was I wasn't doing the work. After losing Ma, I buried the hurt. Following my divorce, I moved on as if everything would fall into place—as my family had thought would happen after Ma died. After leaving the paper, I didn't fight to go back, demanding something better. I never processed any of it. During those two years with Henry, I came out, built my community around him, *his* family, and *his* friends. It all went away with him.

This became my moment of suspension. My future hung below— not above or forward, but *below*—in a black hole of nothingness. I know now an uncertain future can feel like that at times—and I wonder why. After all, just by chance, the future may hold a good deal of peace and happiness, too.

If someone asked, "How are you?" water brimmed up to my eyes. I cried every chance I got—in ladies room stalls, in my car, on walks at lunchtime. The Wall Banger's fist to walls hit the tender spot in my chest, too. Some days I'd arise from it, feeling elated only to find myself the next day at pit bottom without a rope to pull myself up or the strength if I had one.

Depression acted cunning. It hijacked a factor, an excuse to hide in—making me delusional about the origin of my misery. My circumstances planted, cultivated, and grew my grief, I thought. That I held the power to weed the sadness out of myself. If only I had more of this, less of that, a different one of those, well, then, all would be well.

Depression dropped me off in a strange city, without a map or a guide, foreign language dictionary, or tips about what part of town to avoid. Skills or intuition to navigate the turmoil? Clueless. Courage to get out there and place that new stake in the ground? Nope. Instead, I walked in fear, kept my head low, everything in, hoping after swallowing the shock, my body would somehow digest it away.

A few months later, Henry's name popped up on my caller ID.

"You'll never guess who I'm seeing," he said.

"You're seeing someone already?" I asked. I could feel contents of my intestines begin loosening.

"Yes, it's so weird. Do you remember Nancy?" he asked, breaking into a slight giggle.

"You mean Nancy who lives above your cousin's flower shop?" I asked. I met her a couple of times while we were dating. She rented a place from his brother. She with her long wavy red hair and gorgeous figure. She, a single mother with a young son. A boy, for whom, thinking of my own sons, I purchased a Spiderman action figure one time.

"Yes," he said, laughing aloud, smitten with his new love, a girl some ten years younger than me, about twenty years younger than him, by then in his fifties. He didn't love me. I must have been stupid not to see it coming.

"Henry, I have to go."

His call tore off my scabs, leaving my wounds exposed, sticky, and burning. Perhaps I should have deleted him from my phone, from my mind. I wasn't ready. Instead, I changed his name in my phone to "Fool Calling."

Over weeks, the heat in my chest settled into a chronic ache in there. Pain had insidiously grown to become a part of me. I obsessed over my flaws. My imperfect body (if I were a horse with my legs, I would be a Clydesdale, not a thoroughbred). My lack of education ("behind"). My home (attached to the Wall Banger's). My social life (zilch). My job (sold out).

I trembled from the core. Wherever I went, whatever I did, pain flowed along, too. It hung around like that unwelcome kid on the playground.

One day sensing my sadness, Geoff asked "Mom, what's wrong?"

"I'm just sad because Henry and I broke up," I said.

"I'm sorry, Mom," he said.

"It's okay. It will be like I have the flu for a little while. Then I will get better, okay?" I said.

"Okay," he said.

Some relief came from writing, as if pain eased out through ink onto white spaces. So night after night, along with my self-improvement lists, I took my journal to bed and poured my misery onto its pages. I also stopped midday and wrote—at work during a meeting, during college history lessons, between notes on the Bolshevik Revolution, or parked outside ball fields waiting for the boys to finish practice.

"Today the pain has seeped down from my lower chest to the top of my stomach. I feel mildly sick and very sad. I'm so tired of sadness. I don't want to be sad anymore. It's hard to be someone no one wants. Who no worthy person wants. I don't call him or write to him because I couldn't bear the rejection. In this state of deep neediness, what can I do? I will say a prayer for him, and for myself."

Every night, the blows from the other side of our wall came. *Bang! Bang! Bang!* My heart sank deeper.

We'd been living on the other side of the Wall Banger for more than a couple of years. There were just two bedrooms in our place. Geoff asked several times for his own room. A builder assessed our unit for an addition and said it wouldn't work. Meantime, the phone lit up every week or so announcing, *Fool Calling.*

"Hello?" I said.

"Hello," he said.

"Why are you calling me?" I asked.

"I'm just calling to see how you are," he replied.

"I'm okay. Are you still seeing Nancy?" I asked.

"Yes, she just left," he said.

I ended the call. I sometimes welcomed his calls. His voice sang like a favorite song.

Still, those interruptions set me back. I started seeing a therapist during Tuesday lunch hours. On her recommendation, I asked Henry to stop calling. He still did.

One night Geoff reciprocated the wall banging, slamming the short side of his fist to the wall three times, returning powerful blows their way. My sorrowful heart chuckled its first laugh in months. Yet my maternal alarms went off. I didn't raise kids to communicate in primitive code. It was time to go. I couldn't get what I needed most from that house. To feel at home.

Chapter 12

In springtime 2004, brokenhearted and three years into life after divorce, I went house hunting again. Running down my list of requirements, I doubted whether I could afford my then dreamhouse. A single-family home. Something local so the boys could attend the same schools. Three bedrooms. Room for workout equipment. A yard large enough for Greg to kick his soccer ball. A place for Geoff to play his guitar. It was an electric guitar. He was fifteen. He played "hard core."

Most houses in new developments were colonials. Housing development upon housing development crowded with neighbors, bare of trees. Each just another Dr. Seuss *Whoville* of colonials—all designed from the same mold. While those places were similar to what we had pre-divorce, I couldn't bear them anymore. I felt naked, exposed. Seeking something more insular, I desired trees and space. A place with heart and soul. I needed something different. I felt different. I *was* different now.

My realtor, Lisa, called saying she found something I might like about ten minutes from Wall Banger condo.

"It's an older place, three to five bedrooms, two baths, big yard," she explained. "It's just got 'you' written all over it, and it's in your price range."

We agreed to meet there that afternoon. It was pouring rain. I arrived first. Leaned out of my car, popped open my umbrella, and began exploring the yard alone. Rain *tap-tap-tapping* on my umbrella. I could tell. Someone had once loved the place, but no longer did, or could. A vintage gambrel farmhouse with a paned-glass bow window.

A small half-circle room at the front. The roof of that half-circle room spiraled into a pyramid. A finial covered in pale green patina rested on top.

What a shame paint peeled off the house. The rock driveway showed vast areas of dirt where weeds thrived. Chipmunks sped in and out from the broken bottom of a garage door. Stones went this way and that in the warped cobblestone apron at the driveway's entrance.

A short black wrought iron fence—albeit a bit rusted—encased the front yard. I climbed three stone steps to a flagstone walkway that carried me to the front stone stoop, crumbled and overgrown with moss. A garden on either side of the steps greeted me, showing off dying broom plants, overgrown hollies, boxwoods, and other shrubs, as well as weeds invading strawberry plants. Still though, somehow it *did* greet me. In other parts of the yard, ancient, thick vines had grown woody and braided themselves into twisted ropes, strangling neighboring trees and shrubs. Two ancient stone patios. A shabby elegance drew me in. We had one thing in common, this house and me. We were each a little bit broken.

"Sorry, I'm late," said Lisa as she rose from her car.

"Hey, no problem," I said. "I've been checking out the yard."

She struggled with the lock box on the doorknob. "I hope they took their dogs with them," she said, wiggling the key.

The door squealed out a hello. As I walked in for the first time, I felt the home's warm shelter from that cold rain outside. The house wrapped me in a sunny-orange glow and gave me a grandpa hug. Everything, from its paned-glass cabinetry and artisan moldings to its arched doorways and log cabin oak floors, lifted their eyes, gazed my way, and whispered, "It's all right, dear. You're home again."

And it felt that way every time I walked in.

Before deciding to buy the place, I brought the boys over to see it. They bolted upstairs and flew back down, announcing dibs on bedrooms. They scurried outside and explored the yard and hidden walkways. Running back in, they proclaimed their love, and asked when we could move in.

I figured it best to run the idea by Brian, too, since our kids would live there with me.

"So what do you think?" I asked

"I'm going to tell you the truth. I think it's too much work," he said.

"But I think it's a gem," I said. "Look at the yard—it's perfect for the kids."

"Well, you asked me what I think and I'm telling you. I think you should reconsider," he said.

Back then, if I could have foreseen the major punch list of repairs, it would have read like this:

#1: Install proper heating upstairs to avoid gas poisoning boys.
#2: Re-cement decaying front stoop.
#3: Find out why's it's always breezy inside.
#4: Fix gaping hole in siding.
#5: Stop indoor tsunami.
#6: Repair poop pump.
#7: Restore broken garage doors and peanut brittle apron in front of them.

But I was in love.

This place could have fit in along the outskirts of an English village. But rather than a quaint cobblestone road in Tissington, Derbyshire, it sat on a busy asphalt street in Whitinsville, Massachusetts.

The stone patios worked perfectly for evening cookouts and lazy Sunday mornings with coffees and papers. One was made of stone and graced by a purple lilac, a dowager so tall it competed for sun with an ancient maple across from it. A number of fat variegated hosta plants softened edges of this patio.

Then a thick screening of trees and bushes privatized this refuge from traffic. A living art performance appeared in that yard each spring. First the apple tree mushroomed into deep pink. After all its blossoms fell, creating a crimson moat around it, the lilac delivered delicate purple cones. Two weeks later, its mini blossoms wilted as billions of tiny white fragrant flowers on opposite bushes made their debut. This graceful progression of extraordinary blooms must have been orchestrated by someone who loved the place many years ago.

The patio near the house remained empty except for a few pots. It was constructed of brick laid at an incline slightly toward the foundation, rather than slightly away from it—as it should have been. That's why this patio flooded when rains came or snow melted. Some architectural secret or maybe just good fortune kept water from seeping into our basement.

Elsewhere in the yard, an American flag swung its faded red, white, and blue from a rusty white pole as tall as one in a public schoolyard. Iron eagles mounted on the outside of our chimney hinted again at some prior owner's patriotism.

What about a structure makes a good home, anyway? Beyond a shelter, I think it's a private place to which we retreat, one from which we gain sustenance for facing all life inevitably brings—and takes. I feel either let down or built up by the standards of my homes. In many ways, I have become who I am from all the places I've called home. But only here did my home reflect who I had been and who I wished to be.

• • •

Punch List Item #1 – Install proper heating upstairs to avoid gas poisoning boys.

The house came with a small kitchen upstairs, a remnant from its short era as a two-family home. This little galley contained a sink, a well-worn countertop, and shockingly, a propane gas stove. This upstairs kitchen opened through an arch into a dining area with two built-in china cupboards.

The gas stove heated upstairs. Imagining the variety of temptations a stove posed for teenage boys, I hired a carpenter to rip out the old kitchen and refinish walls around it after a plumber capped the pipes inside. Then an electrician installed electric heating baseboards in each upstairs room. Without fail, each contractor asked, "Didn't Susie Yanka once live here?"

I wasn't sure.

I anticipated the cost of the repairs before signing papers. Carved a portion of proceeds from Wall Banger condo.

With the kitchen gone, this space became a perfect bedroom for Geoff. We kept that wide arch opening. Painters made his walls sky blue, painting the nook a hue darker. Geoff and I moved his desk and chest of drawers into the little nook where that kitchen had been. We fit his bed, nightstand, and armoire in the remaining space. Installed some blue plaid curtains and tossed out a matching bedspread.

I didn't know then Geoff would spend only a brief four to five years of his life in that room. Once he went to college, he never returned home, except for weeks between apartments. Still, that little blue room hosted his band practices and became a respite from what might plague teenage boys and from long days, too, working as a paintball field referee.

Knock, knock.

"Goodnight, Geoff. I love you," I'd call through his door.

"Goodnight, Mom. I love you, too," he'd always say.

• • •

Before that place, it had been a long time since I'd *really* been home—in my own corner of sanctuary. My soul's bed and an expression of my passions, home holds all that's uniquely me. It's where I rest, reflect, and grow. As good or as bad as they've been, the homes I've known share a place in my heart where ex-lovers, lost relatives, and estranged friends live. Most of all, I believe home is a place to which we should always feel welcome to return.

Chapter 13

We'd been living in our vintage house for about a year. My internal con artist, depression, was wrong. Buying a house didn't cancel my sadness, but something therapeutic began happening. Outside one spring day in 2005, I wrestled with a broken weed whacker. After managing to get it working, I swung it too close to myself, sending debris into my ankles at the speed of sparks. The little beast chewed up all its string before I finished. I held the brat upside down. Struggled with reloading the thick plastic spaghetti into its cartridge like dental floss back into its container. Amid all this, a strange car pulled up the driveway.

Weed whacker in hand, I approached the closest door—on the passenger's side. An elderly woman looked up at me, and said, "My name is Pauline Bailey. I am eighty-eight years old, and I used to live here when I was a little girl."

The driver leaned over and introduced herself as Pauline's daughter. Sprinkling in apologies for stopping by without an invitation, she mentioned that while visiting a nearby relative, her mother asked about seeing inside her childhood home again.

I dropped the machine, brushed grass off my pants, and invited Pauline and her daughter in. Pauline stood tall and thin and a bit hunched in 1960's-Saturday-casual. Short stylish white hair. Crisp, white blouse under beige boiled wool jacket. Beige waist-high pants. Kelly-green Keds. As she walked, every now and then she'd sway, become a bit off balance, but then catch her footing. She had that humble way about her people seem to acquire after years of challenge, failure, will, then finally, success or better yet, grace.

As we approached my back door, my mind prioritized questions about the place. "Was it really built in 1930? How long did the original owners live here? What were they like and what happened to them?"

I opened the door leading to the mudroom. My home's messes became most apparent just before company arrived. As we entered the mudroom, what did we see? Shoes. Running shoes, skateboard shoes, lawn-cutting shoes, golf shoes, baseball and soccer cleats, flip flops, and loafers, and a pair or two of high heels thrown in.

"Please excuse the mess," I said.

"Oh, don't worry about that," she said.

On good days, most shoes stayed stashed in what had been a textile worker's tool trunk. On decent days, shoes sat organized in neat rows. On bad days, they became strewn about, shoes this way, shoes that way, requiring us to hunt down and reunite a pair before going out. Pauline arrived on a bad shoe day. I felt embarrassed, partly for the mess, but mostly for our consumption.

"It's just my boys need a place to come in, before they come in," I said. Pauline and her daughter laughed.

She asked their ages. I said they were twelve and fifteen.

"There are just two boys," I said. "But you'd think I had six by looking at this room."

Enduring a century of foot traffic, the mudroom looked tired. Trying various do-it-yourself improvements—painting over dull stenciling, installing cheap linoleum—I'd concluded the only real enhancement required ripping it off the house, and rebuilding it altogether. Perhaps replacing it with a classy little sunroom. However, every time I presented such ideas to my budget, it stared back at me like a husband.

Despite my shame, Pauline walked right through this shanty and into the kitchen without stopping, like she'd probably done all her life in that house, anxious for dinner, phone time, or just refuge from the world outside. Of course, today, she seemed anxious to reminisce. So was I.

After all, as homeowners, we get only a vague sense of the people who inhabited our places before us from indelible clues they leave behind—say, hand-crafted molding, a springtime choreography of flowering trees, or some hint of patriotism. Like a distant cousin's shoddy scrapbook, a house strives to tell you about its prior people. But no need for the house to talk this day. One of its priors had shown up to speak for herself. As we walked in, Midnight trotted over, and sensing our guests' disinterest, retreated back to her bed in another room.

Pauline glanced around my kitchen like a child on her first field trip to the local fire station. Hand built mustard cupboards. Glass front cabinet doors. Shelves shaped like chapel windows. A simple vintage black iron chandelier over a breakfast bar.

"It looks the same," she said.

Pointing out a cabinet under the chapel-window shelves, she said, "That's where we kept the family Bible. We took it out each day to say our prayers. That's how my father taught himself English. He came here from a little town in Holland called Friesland."

"In what year was this house built, Pauline?" I asked.

Her lips moved like silent prayers as she considered her age, the number of years she'd lived there, then the math.

"It must have been about 1923," she said. "My father built this house. I remember helping him to bang in the nails. I must have been about six years old."

In my garage and basement, they left behind some remarkable workbenches, enormous and made of heavy wood, with built-in shelves, drawers, and thick surfaces, all scarred and indented. Small circles, where perhaps some pipe was held steady and whacked with a hammer; gouges where some screwdriver slid off target and met the bench instead; several deep scratches in a neat row, where perhaps a vice grip was mounted, all this but still a surface strong enough to endure more. Dad would have been impressed.

I said, "I heard this house was built by a man named Osterman. I get the impression he was quite a craftsman."

Pauline looked at me, like I'd just delivered important news, and gave a solemn nod.

"He worked on and off at Whitin Machine Works—in the mill's box shop," she explained.

Pronounced "white-tin," Whitin Machine Works inhabited the mill building located at the bottom of my street, about two and a half miles away. Author Jeanne Schinto said, "If you were to take the Empire State

Building and lay it sideways, you'd have the Lawrence mill." Same is true of old Whitin mill, with its red brick and hundreds of windows in three straight rows, stretching a good length along Main Street. From what I've gathered, box shop workers built cabinetry and also boxes to ship the mill machinery that the company produced.

Walking from the kitchen, Pauline led me into our den, which opened into the dining room. A long radiator kept our living room toasty warm during winters. Four windows overlooked the side yard. A door led outside from this room.

"This room used to be a porch," Pauline said. "Then my father made it part of the main house. He was always doing something around here."

At that time, we had a green tartan plaid couch and matching love seat in there, a large wide-board coffee table, and an armoire housing the television, all compliments of a life we lived before divorce.

In this room, the boys hung out with friends, watched television, played video games, and sometimes during the darkness of night, whispered secrets. Geoff restrung and played his guitar in that room. I caught him taking apart a skateboard in there once. This room served more as a respite than a workspace for Greg, who spent many quiet evenings stretched out on the couch recovering from multiple athletics.

"My sister, my mother, and I waxed these floors on our hands and knees once a year," Pauline said. "It was a lot of work."

She gave me another wide-eyed serious stare, planting her words as a reminder to take care of my floors.

"No wonder these floors are in such good shape today. I have never waxed them, not ever," I admitted.

Looking at the living room floor, Pauline asked, "Is the secret board still there?"

"You mean that part of floor that lifts out?" I asked, pointing to a section of floorboard.

"Yes, that's it," she said. "My father hid fifty-dollar bills in there. He was saving to take my mother to Washington (state)."

"Did they go?" I asked.

"He died before he could take her, but my brother took her later on," she said.

Discovering this hidey-hole by accident a year earlier, I wondered what it was. As I dusted our coffee table and walked over this section of floor, it went, *ba-boop*, like a chair with a short leg when you sit on it. I stood on it and leaned this way and that. *Ba-boop*. And again. *Ba-boop*. I studied the floor, then saw camouflaged within its log-cabin pattern, a rectangular cut-out, about three by four feet. I rushed into the kitchen and grabbed a butter knife. Then using it as a lever, I eased the board out. Its scent hinted of cedar. I figured it was a crawl space for wiring, fit the removeable floor piece back in, and forgot about it—until Pauline's visit.

As she spoke, I studied the floor and watched Ma remove the landscape painting from the wall, turn the dial a smidgen this way and that, and place envelopes into a safe—paychecks for Dad's employees.

Pauline glanced over at our dining room. This faint yellow room settled itself into a perfect little square space and served as a throughway to the parlor in one direction and our bathroom and my bedroom in another. White woodwork and a chair rail. A large vintage floral print I found at an antique festival on the wall.

Running a hand along the molding of a built-in china cupboard, she said, "This used to be an entrance to a staircase. My father removed the staircase to make that room bigger." Pauline pointed to the parlor behind the cupboard. "He salvaged the staircase doorway and its wooden moldings to build this cupboard."

"That's amazing. I never would have guessed that," I said, running my hand along the molding, too.

I examined its glass doors on top and three wooden drawers underneath. I had seen this cupboard hundreds of times. Heck, I lined its shelves in lace and on them, stacked what few decorative dishes I owned. With a backstory, the cupboard became something more—a sort of heirloom.

"He built that one, too," she said, pointing to a cupboard built into the opposite corner.

The table in that room accompanied me for more than thirty years. As a newlywed shopping with my then husband, I pointed to it, and said, "That one." Round and constructed of solid maple, it had matching Windsor chairs. My table survived scratches from skateboards parked and sandwiches cut on it while I wasn't home, and to be fair, the candle wax and cup rings I contributed to its surface.

Through early marriage romance, joy in bringing each new baby home, more holidays and family dinners than I can count. Enduring spit up, bitter divorce, midnights dabbed by misguided glue-sticks aimed at construction paper. Through many bursts of, "Never put new shoes on the table," and worrisome discussions over this trouble and that one, the aging maple table stood strong for me.

Pauline and I made our way around the table, across the dining room, and into our wide, square hallway outside the bathroom. Peering into the bathroom, she observed the floor of tiny black and white ceramic tiles, walls of larger black and white tiles, a white cast iron tub, and my favorite, an extra-large tile of pink flamingos, smack in the middle of our shower wall.

"It's all the same," she said. Then laughing, she added, "My sister and I hung out that window smoking cigarettes."

"But there's no window," I said.

"There was a window right there," she said, pointing to a large mirror above my toilet.

I managed to lift the mirror inches from the wall and sure enough, there it was: a window! Through its dusty glass panes I could see a sheet of wood behind it. While at first, I felt disappointed by the shoddy work—that no one bothered removing that window and rebuilding the wall—I grew to appreciate it as another of my home's quirky little secrets, like the hidey-hole. And its presence increased my home's value a bit more, at least for me.

Back on our tour, we made our way past our bathroom, to my bedroom. Making my bed required walking sideways alongside one wall. Stacks of books waited on the floor—overflow from my night table. My bedroom had three windows on one side and one on another wall, which overlooked Mary Army's home.

"Did you know the Armys?" I asked Pauline.

"No, I don't remember them," she said.

"Mary Army must be in her seventies. On warm days, she walks in her yard barefoot, tending her gardens and chickens," I said. "She leaves cartons of eggs on our doorstep, and sometimes day-old baked goods—senior center donation leftovers."

"We had chickens, too," Pauline said. "My grandparents owned a farm down the road. They lost it during the Depression, so my father built this room for them. My grandparents stayed here for two years while my father built that house next door for them."

"Mrs. Army's house or the cottage behind this one?" I asked.

"No, on the other side of this house," she said.

Walking from my boudoir, Pauline didn't ask about the other downstairs bedroom. That likely had been her parents'. It contained my workout equipment the day Pauline visited, and later, my office. We returned past the bathroom, across the hallway, back through dining room territory, into my parlor.

A brick fireplace, which someone painted sage green owned this room. Its white wooden mantel held a few candles and a stack of three books—Nicholas Evans' *The Horse Whisperer*, V. Sackville-West's *In Your Garden*, and a Harvard Classics titled *Letters and Treatises of Cicero and Pliny*. Standing in the parlor, we looked through the front bow window, which framed Mr. and Mrs. Susienka's vintage cape and tidy yard opposite mine. Keep in mind, *Susienka* is pronounced Susie-yank-a. Never hearing this name before, when contractors asked me, *Didn't Susienka used to live here*, I assumed a woman whose first name was *Susie* and whose last name was *Yanka* must have lived in my house. Meeting this lovely older couple clarified everything. Their son had purchased my place from the Osterman estate and lived here for just a short time.

Probably in her eighties, Mrs. Susienka stands about five-foot-four. She always gazed at me through compassionate eyes. She first welcomed us to the neighborhood with a homemade Dutch apple pie, saying one-crust pies made using canola oil were easier on the heart. She explained the crust's recipe was simple. One-third cup of canola oil, one-third cup of flour, one-third cup of sugar. "Just remember a therd, a therd, and a therd," she said.

Mr. Susienka is probably in his eighties and stands more than six-feet tall. His eyes and smile collaborate in a way that convey he's always telling an innocent truth. Mr. Susienka catches cool water running from his shower into a bucket while it warms and uses that water for his vegetable garden—a small square patch, chock full of everything edible that will grow during a New England summer. He used to leave summer squash, tomatoes, and Swiss chard in plastic Shaw's bags on my door handle. As I lay awake on summer weekend mornings, I often heard Mr. Susienka's polka music ever so faintly through my bedroom window screen. Every morning, he raised the American flag in his front yard. At dusk, he'd be out there again, hand over hand, pulling it down.

One evening I stopped by their place to borrow a book about Whitin mill. Standing in their den, I watched Mr. Susienka open his woodstove door and nudge a glowing log using an iron poker while his wife pulled the book from a shelf. She opened it. "See," she said, pointing at an image of women packing items like mini Goodyear blimps into boxes.

"During World War II, they made bombs for the war right down here at Whitin mill," she said.

As I left, Mr. Susienka insisted on walking me home even though it took only about a dozen steps to cross over from his house. Facing my house that night, I observed my dining room chandelier for the first time from the street—centered in my front bow window, glistening like a herd of fireflies. I fell deeper in love.

Back on our tour, Pauline didn't ask about going upstairs. Fearing exposé of my sons' bedrooms, I didn't offer to take her there. By this time, she apologized for bothering me, while I assured her it had been my pleasure. She and her daughter refused my relentless offers to stay for tea. We stepped back into fresh air and were greeted by the lilac's fragrance. She said her mother had planted it as a sapling.

Walking back to the car, Pauline pointed out where one of her mother's gardens had been—a semi-circle abutting a patio. She said her father had built a wooden arbor. It stood over the two stone steps before the patio. We scanned the property and discovered the grey-weathered structure leaning against a decrepit shed, all snarled in twisted vines. I told her I would disentangle it and put it back in its original spot. She gave me another earnest nod. But I changed my mind as the words spilled from my mouth, considering the move would splinter it to pieces.

I asked Pauline to wait while I ran in and grabbed a pen and paper to get her address.

When I came back out, I managed one last question. Pointing to the flagpole, its withering American flag flailing like a skinny guy holding on in the wind. "Did your family put up that flagpole?"

"My father did," she said. "My brothers fought during World War II. Both came home. My father put that up when the first one went off to war."

I'd meant to take the old pole down, what, with the rust and all. But after learning its backstory, I decided to keep it just as it was. Another heirloom.

As Pauline settled into the car, I yanked a generous bouquet of purple lilacs from her mother's tree and handed them to her. After their car drove off, I grabbed a lilac bouquet for myself, placed it in a mason jar of water, and set it on my dining room table. On hands and knees, peering into darkness under my bed, I reached in and dug out the white Bible Eleanor gave me for my confirmation. Dusted it off and thumbed through it. Something fell out onto the floor—a folded white paper containing a list I had scribbled in purple ink. I unfolded and read it:

1. *We love each other.*
2. *Good role model for boys (responsible, strong, balanced).*
3. *No active addictions. [The word "active" was inserted later.]*
4. *Dependable (or calls if can't make it).*
4. *Jolly and good natured.*
[There are two #4s—I guess I give equal weight to dependability and joviality.]
5. *Good listener.*
6. *Decisive/can take control.*
7. *Smart and likes to read.*
8. *Have interests in common.*

I had forgotten about that list. Several years before, a therapist advised me to put more thought into my choices of men and suggested I develop a list of qualities I'd like in a partner, and place that list into my Bible. At first, I thought it a peculiar place for such a list, then supposed it's the sort of thing a woman should keep sacred.

Acknowledging I still hadn't found him, I tucked the list back inside, and placed my Bible into its new blessed home—the same cabinet where the Osterman family had kept theirs.

• • •

Punch List Item #2 – Re-cement decaying front stoop.

I met Mike and a group of other writing students in the lobby of a Brown University campus building. He was fifty-something. I was forty-something. We were there for a week-long writers' symposium, an intensive five-day program presented by Brown instructors on life stories. It must have been about 2005. July. Mike has primary lateral sclerosis, a motor neuron disease that is gradually weakening his muscles. When I first met him, he managed with a cane and soon after with a walker he later named Johnnie Walker.

Since the Brown symposium, Mike and I have shared a friendship over writing, sometimes attending other workshops and critiquing each other's work. We go for dinner or drinks a couple times a year. It's not a romance thing. Mike's married. He and his wife Anna share a contemporary home overlooking Kickemuit River on the Rhode Island coast.

Mike is a Renaissance man. He said he did a bunch of drugs during his younger years. Today Mike prefers bourbon and cigars. He built high-end furniture. Owned a couple successful businesses, last of which was an environmental dangerous-waste management company. When pulled over for speeding, he sometimes flashed a silver embossed badge to state troopers. The origin of the badge remains a bit of a mystery. I don't ask questions.

As a writer, Mike spends abundant time in his man cave crafting stories. He blogs, wins awards, and publishes essays in literary magazines. I get the idea he can crack just about anything.

"What's wrong with your front stoop?" he asked when he came to get me for a writing workshop in Boston.

"The top is chipped and broken. A mason estimated a few grand to replace it," I said. "So it's on the punch list."

"We could fix that for under a hundred bucks," he said.

I studied his face, trying to imagine a person needing a walker using power tools, pouring cement, and setting in new tile.

"I could never let you do that," I said.

"You help me, and we'll do it next Saturday," he said.

"Seriously?" I replied.

It was warm and sunny the day Mike arrived to work on the stoop. A black bag in his trunk contained a power saw, hammer, trowel, and other tools. In my garage, I watched him. On his knees, he banged scrap wood together using a hammer and nails to make footings for a cement form. Then he threw a hammer, the footings, and a fifty-pound bag of cement into a wheelbarrow. It was my job to get the wheelbarrow down the gravel driveway to the stoop. It was Mike's job to get down the driveway. He didn't want help. He shuffled, using his arms as much as his legs to maneuver Johnnie Walker's wheels over the pebbles, then up three steps to the flagstone walkway that led to the stoop. Once there, he abandoned the walker and crawled up the steps toward my broken stoop.

He wiped his brow. I felt guilty.

An hour into our job, between a series of "hand me thises" and "hand me thats," he said, "You know when you're really dead?"

"When?" I asked.

He motioned for me to pass him a garden hose.

"When people forget about you," he said.

I poured powdered cement into the wheelbarrow, cocking my head away from dust. He doused it with water.

"I think as long as you're alive in someone's memory, you still exist," he said.

I mixed the cement with an old wooden spoon.

"The real end is when everything about you is forgotten," he said.

He placed footings around the stoop and banged them into place. I handed him bucketfuls of cement. He poured the grey slop into the form. It took us about three Saturdays to complete the job, fitting new tiles into place on top. It looked beautiful and should last a long time.

• • •

I still think about what Mike said. There is so much of Ma that lives on through me. Ma and I shopped in a small convenience store, a *five and dime* as they were called back then. I was about four- or five-years-old. While Ma sorted through goods, I helped myself to a Reese's Peanut Butter Cup. Glancing over, Ma's face turned downward in discovering the chocolate on my mouth and the wrapper in my hand.

She took my arm and rushed me over to the cashier. Told me to explain what I'd done and pay for the candy as she passed me change to hand over. Embarrassed about my theft in the car coming home, I asked her not to tell anyone. She promised she wouldn't. Then she told Dorothea—and I felt even more ashamed.

Decades later as a mother with Geoff as a five-year-old at Macy's, I experienced a similar incident. While I perused merchandise nearby, he explored Christmas ornaments on a display tree. I heard a crash and shot a look at Geoff who was staring down.

"It was an accident, Mom," he said.

"I know," I said, studying the shattered glass. "But we still have to pay for it."

I picked up as many pieces as I could manage and handed him some dollar bills. I took his hand, like Ma did with me, and wandered around, searching for the cashier. I had Geoff explain and hand over money to pay for it. This cashier didn't take the money, though. Still, Geoff seemed to feel good about confessing.

Obviously, Ma's pain lives on through me, but so does her grace. Perhaps it will live on through the boys, and their children someday, too. That ought to keep Ma alive for generations to come.

Chapter 14

My meditations on Ma come mostly following visits to my childhood home. Like Pauline, I return as an adult, too—often since Dorothea still lives there—in that same apartment Dad created years ago after one of his umpteen splits with Eleanor. Virgin Mary vanished long ago. Grass grew over that path between our house and my grandparents', so much so, no one would guess the little trail was ever there. Tall weeds conquered the alcove where I hid and played. Short walls comprising it cracked and crumbled. Looking at that cubby now, there's no hint telling it served as a little hideaway for children long ago. The dirt driveway that horseshoes up and around the house is rutted from erosion due to raining, freezing, and thawing over the decades since Ma died. It's a bumpy ride up to and away from that house.

My pain over losing Ma is like that path, alcove, and driveway—overrun and decayed by all that's happened since she died. My mind still sometimes summons water to my eyes, a lump to my throat, and ache to my heart, just for Ma. These come unexpectedly now and then. Maybe it's a song on the radio, a relative's kind words. Something I read. Something I see. Whatever trigger, the water, the lump, the heat in my chest, these symptoms of loss hibernate inside me—questions to aunties whose words can't soothe. A cold mattress with my jacket and clothes on. A new family, then oops, nope, no new family. A frozen best friend at the end of a mean chain on a bitter cold winter day, just yards from a toasty warm house. The heroin my brother pumped into his veins. The Bad Lady at the Fernald School. Dorothea's stifled life. Words Michael and Andy never shared about what they witnessed in our basement that day. These events sleep in the overgrown weeds and ruts of my mind.

Since I left my childhood home for good, carpenters replaced the rickety wooden door with a fiberglass one and widened the entrance, easing the way for Donnie's wheelchair. My brother started needing the chair about a decade ago. Donnie can walk, albeit with a walker, from bedroom to kitchen and back. He uses the wheelchair for longer jaunts. Workers enlarged the downstairs bathroom and its doorway so he can maneuver around corners. The carpenters remodeled Donnie's bedroom for similar reasons, adding a larger door, new wooden floor, wallpaper, and furniture. The upstairs where I shared an apartment with Dad and Michael remains unoccupied and dilapidated due to busted pipes.

When I arrive, rather than "Welcome home, Dear," this house seems to say, "Oh, it's you again."

Dorothea and Bob's son, Todd, left the nest and married years ago. As I walk in, Dorothea greets me with a warm smile and a hug and tells me how happy she is to see me. Bob smiles and makes some wise crack like, "Did you come to take me out on a date?"

During one visit in about springtime 2006, Donnie shuffled out to see me.

"Hallo Meg-gayle! Did you bring me pichas?" he asked.

He long ago grew bored of baseball. He moved on to World Wrestling Federation matches, got sick of that, and has since become obsessed over photographs and junk mail. If I remember, that is, if I am wise, I will bring him the pictures and mail. Of anyone, of anything. Otherwise, he will pester me for them during my entire visit. Though he can't read, he appreciates when I bring him take-out menus, flyers, promotional literature—glossy and printed on card stock. Doesn't matter what it's for—gutter replacement, new salon grand openings, expired coupons, dental appointment reminders, etcetera. New pictures and junk mail satiate his fix for the stuff. He piles hours upon hours every day sorting through his papers and pictures. He clasps a stack of them like a defense attorney in court holding case notes and transports his pictures from room to room in a little metal basket on his walker.

That time, I brought him a few new pictures of Geoff and Greg. We sat at Dorothea's table. He studied each one as a collector examines a rare pamphlet. Then he gathered the pictures from his basket. Placed them on the table. One by one, he chose a picture from his pile, placed it before himself and pointed at faces. Said their names.

"Dat's Michael," he said, putting his index figure on Michael's face. "Where's Michael?"

I answered him how I always do these days. "Michael's in heaven."

"With Daaad?" Donnie asked.

"Yes, with Dad," I said.

"I miss Michael," he said. Wearing a pout, he searched my face for some resolution.

"I do, too, Don," I said.

Michael died of a heart attack a year earlier, a couple weeks shy of his forty-seventh birthday. Michael's eighteen-year-old son found him lying on Dad's camper floor. Michael had married Bessie, a girl who, in a tantrum, burned Teddy, his favorite childhood toy, on the walkway outside the old house. When Michael died, they had been divorced several years. He had sold his house not long after and managed losing most of his money, despite having Dad's garage. That's what led to his living in the camper, like Dad did sometimes when he left Eleanor. When I think of Michael, I can't help thinking how Ma was about the same age when she died—almost forty-four—and that Michael's son found him dead, like Michael had found Ma dead. I still can't believe sometimes that Michael already left us.

Donnie chose another picture from his pile.

"Dat's JacKieeeeeee," he said. There remain layers packed into Donnie's annunciation of Jackie's name—making an extra hard k sound and holding the long e for an extra-long time, all in a mischievous tone. Then he reads my face for a reaction before picking up the next image from his pile.

We have underestimated Donnie's ability to comprehend crises. Despite his intellectual disability, Donnie remains astute in family matters. He has witnessed our hardships, like an informant sweeping a sidewalk observes an unsuspecting criminal. Donnie discerns topics we only dance around in his presence, including the complexities of our relationships and family dysfunction.

Over the years, Jackie went on and off dope and in and out of treatment centers. During the good years, this second-oldest brother married and had a son, Chris, the one who towed Dad's hearse, body and all, to the cemetery on a ramp truck. During the bad years, Jackie falsified our checks, stole our possessions, begged us for money, and attempted blackmailing us if we refused handing it over. Like my other siblings, I avoided such trouble by remaining estranged from Jackie. I saw him last at Michael's funeral. We were cordial and kind, hugging in pain of our shared loss. Jackie died of a heart attack at sixty-four in 2012.

Jackie adored Donnie and remained kind and playful toward him. For that, Donnie remembers him fondly. However, Donnie also remains keen to the grief Jackie caused everyone else over the years. It wouldn't surprise me if Donnie articulated some of the specifics. I just don't ask.

"Who's that, Donnie?" I said as he picked up the next picture.

"Dat's Andy," he said. "Where's Andy?"

"Andy's working," I said.

Andy died at seventy-four in a tragic fall during 2017. Before then, Andy and I saw each other only occasionally. He had started his own towing and recovery business decades ago—towing tractor trailer and other large-scale vehicles. My oldest brother, Andy, vowed to avoid competing with Dad's car repair shop. Andy surrendered his business to his ex-wife during their divorce. He started another company, selling tow trucks and equipment. Andy and I never discussed how we lost Ma or anything about her. He didn't bring up anything below the surface.

Donnie and I continued sharing his pictures. There were those of Dorothea and Bob, whom he identified as "The Cop" because Bob worked as a security guard back then. There were pictures of Dorothea and Bob's son, Todd, and Todd's then wife, Katie, and *their* son, Tommy. There were pictures of Michael's children, Anne, Anthony, and Stacey. There were pictures of Jackie's son, Christopher, with his children, Christina, Kayleigh, and Andrew, and of my boys and of Bob's relatives. There were laminated memorial prayer cards for Auntie Theresa, Uncle Johnny, and many of our other late aunts and uncles. There were scores of pictures of other people. Strangers. He must have hundreds of pictures. Maybe thousands.

Among them was one picture of Ma, but we didn't see it that day.

I love these moments with Donnie, sharing what he sees in his pictures. However, over my lifetime, I can't count how many times I felt fortunate—and guilty—for being a child when Ma died, escaping the responsibility Dorothea bore. Once I became mature enough to pitch-in in any meaningful way, I didn't.

Off I went to live with Eleanor and Dad. To drink and party. To get married. Have children. Get divorced. Date and drink and party some more. To build a career. To build drama and take time to heal from my drama. I have traveled a bit. To England, Scotland, France, Brazil, and Greece, and up and down and across the United States.

Dorothea never left Donnie's side. Every morning she gets up and runs water for his bath. She kneels beside her tub and scrubs his back. Then he stands in his terry towel wrapped around his chubby waist while she shaves him. He still might stare at his fingers briefly cross-eyed and groan his happy groan. Once dressed, he waddles to her table where she serves him his favorite breakfast: peanut butter on toast and a glass of milk. He goes to his room—the largest and nicest room in her house, the only one with air conditioning—and "works" on his "*papersh*" until lunchtime when he comes out for a chicken sandwich or a burger. He goes back to his papers until dinnertime, then he comes out for a hot meal (his favorite is fried clams), then back until snack time, which comes before bedtime. During a part of every day, he sits cross-legged on his bed for hours, blasting Kenny Rogers' CDs over and over and over and over again, singing along with them loud enough to hear his raspy voice over the music, "You picked a fine time to leave me Lucille ..." or he might watch fake wrestling for more hours. He cannot stay home alone.

Stacks of folded and pressed bright white t-shirts, underwear, socks, and other ironed shirts fill his drawers. Dorothea takes Donnie to his doctor appointments several times a month and counts and organizes his medicines for each day in pill boxes. Donnie's back problems landed him in the hospital at least twice and each time, Dorothea and Bob sat with him for hours a day. Donnie's arms are short. Not so short people notice. But too short for one crucial aspect of personal hygiene. They are too short to wipe his ass. Every time Dorothea hears him sing from the bathroom, "I'm doooo-ne," in a song tone a child playing an outdoor game might use, she stops whatever she's doing and rushes in to clean him. She has done all of this and so much more every single day for more than nineteen thousand and five hundred days since we lost Ma.

I sit with Donnie once a month for ten minutes to run through his pictures and papers. And let me repeat: As I walk into the house, she always greets me with a warm smile and a hug and tells me how happy she is to see me. As a little girl, I thought my sister *looked like* an angel. She was so beautiful. In adulthood, I believe she has become an angel.

Sitting there in my old childhood home, it's impossible to avoid wondering what would have happened if Ma got help—if she'd lived. She'd likely be gone by now, but what if she made it into her golden years? Dorothea would have been free to go off with Bob, maybe build some career or become an artist. And me? What would have become of me? And Donnie? And Michael? Jackie? Andy? Impossible to know. Who knows, too, what other calamity might have met us along those other paths. We'd have all been closer; that's one thing for sure. Through guilt and obligation, holidays and birthdays, support given, and assistance taken, children gather 'round their mothers and might, by default, each other.

After viewing pictures with Donnie, Dorothea and I got caught up over tea at her dining room table. She has aged, as we all have. Her pretty eyes still glow. Bored by our conversation, Donnie collected his pictures and returned to his room. Dorothea and I talked about books we're reading and whatever was happening in our family, and in the news. We sit on opposite sides of politics, so in terms of national and world events, we discuss only the outrageous—only points we can agree on.

"I've been meaning to ask you," I said. "Did Ma ever leave a note?"

"She left three notes, one for Andy, one for Jackie, and one for me. One of our relatives, I don't know who, took them and never let anyone read them," she said.

"You're kidding me," I said. "Do you think we can get them now?"

"No, they're all dead," she said.

Before I left, Dorothea packed me some water for the ride home and handed me a box of cinnamon spice teabags. Even though she and Bob sometimes struggle to get by, she always gives me something for myself or my kids.

I walked down the hallway to Donnie's room and knocked on the door.

"Come in," he called out, like a knight guarding a medieval castle yelling, "Who goes there!"

I walked in. He was sitting on the edge of his bed with his pictures sorted in piles all around him. We hugged.

"Love you, Don," I said.

"I love you, too, Meg-gayle," he said, like he always says, with the sweetest, purest smile a human being can make.

The real emotion came, as these sentiments often come, after my visits, during the hour-long or so drive home. I grabbed a grande decaf first. Hopped on Interstate 495, heading south. No radio. Just me and my thoughts. Sipped coffee. Highway lines blinked by. I dug deep into my memory, trying hard to remember that day Ma died and ones just before it. I questioned whether I have events of that day straight. Ma died on March 21, 1968. The only clear details directly from my own memory come up to the point when I told Ma I peed my bed. Between then and the point when Uncle Johnny knocked on my bedroom door is gone. Everything in that black hole has been reconstructed based on what bits people have said and based on what I know about my family and Ma.

I'd always heard Michael went down to our basement for his skates that day. But who told me that? Then I question if temperatures could have been too warm that March to skate. According to historical weather reports, Massachusetts suffered a bitter cold winter that year. A few days just before Ma died, the air outside turned mild. Scientists say that whether the pond stayed frozen depended on many factors—thickness of the ice, amount of snow covering it, depth of the water beneath the ice, and even whether wind blew during the warm spell. So technically, the pond's ice may have been thick enough to skate on, but was it?

I drove through Westford, Massachusetts, past the exit for Kimball's ice cream where Dad used to take us.

I slept at Auntie Theresa's that first night after Ma died. I remembered heaving a sigh of relief as I lay alone in my cousin's bed that night. Why did I feel relieved? I thought back to a few months before Ma died. One evening Michael, Donnie, and I stayed alone with her as we often did at night. Dad owned racehorses and traveled to horse tracks in southern New Hampshire—from thirty to ninety minutes away. Dorothea dated or went out with friends. Andy was married and on his own. Jackie was who knows where.

That night, Ma ranted and raved about this and about that. I don't know what about. She pounded on Donnie's back. Donnie, at just three years old. On that night of her rant, I tiptoed past the floor's swirly grate up to the threshold of my brothers' bedroom. In my pajamas, I peered through, past piles of clothes strewn across their floor, and through another doorway into the bathroom where I washed my dollies' hair. I wondered why Ma lay on our bathroom floor. She directed Michael to swaddle her inside blankets like a mummy—and he somehow managed it.

I ended up on the sofa by the time paramedics rushed by with Ma on a stretcher. Dorothea's glum face matched the worry in her eyes. The silence among everyone conveyed the *we don't talk about this* we all understood without a word. Ma soon—the next day?—came home and everything seemed fine, as if the rants and the swaddling and the paramedics never happened.

On my drive home, I noticed the Route 2 exit for Walden Pond and reminded myself to visit again sometime, then returned to my meditation on Ma.

There came that time when I had to have been about five. Several rows of thin, red slices covered Ma's wrists.

"Ma, what happened?" I asked.

She said something about trying to divide herself into multiple people, clones to accomplish all her chores. During those rough times, she once told me that one day, I would have a new mother, a younger mother. This terrified me.

"I don't want a younger mother," I cried. "I want you."

We hold no doubt Dad cheated on her—and abused her. During one of my visits, Dorothea mentioned how when I was very small, Dad saw a woman who owned a local bar. One early morning he hadn't returned home yet. Ma stormed over there and banged on the door. Dad came out in an undershirt. Back home, sparks flew, and Ma ended up with a black eye. He never hit Eleanor. Still, Dad had a knack for treating women like second-rate citizens, alive to serve only him and care for his children.

Michael, Donnie, and I didn't attend Ma's funeral. As a child, I don't recall talking with Dad or my siblings about losing Ma. Even teachers and school administrators stayed buttoned up about it. One afternoon in my second-grade class, Mrs. Gray read us a story about a spider and a pig that talked to each other. During the story, I sat with my head on the desk, like many of the other children did at story time. I couldn't follow the narrative, though. As other children laughed or gasped, I had no idea what they were reacting to. My head wasn't in it. I wasn't thinking about Ma. I wasn't thinking. Was that normal?

Years later, exploring books to read to my boys, I came across that familiar cover for *Charlotte's Web* by E.B. White. I bought it and read it to them. In the story Wilbur, a pig, is afraid to die, and Charlotte, a spider, helps to save him from the slaughterhouse. In the end, it is Charlotte who dies—and knows her fate all along. She focuses on living rather than dying and sees her legacy in her egg sac.

After reading *Charlotte's Web* to the boys, I wondered if Mrs. Gray was reading it mainly to me. Unlike Charlotte, I don't think Ma was thinking about her legacy as she stepped down into the basement that day.

No matter, I am hers. She is mine. Whether true or not, I sense that everything good within me originates from her—and what's evil within me, I gathered elsewhere on the way to growing up—something to be ashamed of.

I passed the exit for Bolton. I only recently began etching into the surface of perhaps why Ma "snapped" as I've heard people whisper. By talking with relatives and hearing their occasional commentary about it, I discovered Ma was not psychotic during her childhood or during most of her adult life. Old fashioned maybe, but not nuts.

Ma grew up in Lowell's Centralville neighborhood, where Jack Kerouac was born two years before her. Centralville, or as locals pronounced it, *Cennaville*, became a working-class neighborhood filled with descendants of mill-era immigrants. Ma arrived somewhere in the middle of seven other children. Uncle Sonny described their dad, Pa, as a "hard" man. Pa came from Stonington, Maine. Pa's mother died in childbirth and his father abandoned him. Maybe that's why Pa was a hard man. Ma's mother was a devout Catholic. Her family had immigrated to Leigh Leicestershire, England from Ireland during the potato famine. She emigrated from England to America alone in 1905 at fifteen and worked as a housekeeper. Ma's parents died before my birth. Ma's siblings visited us often. Ma graduated from Lowell High School and worked in a soda shop.

"We met at a roller-skating rink on Central Street in Lowell," Dad said. "I was goin' around tryin-a roller skate. I just kept fallin' down and I said, 'What the hell is goin' on here?' I went to the guy and said, 'I can't stand up. What's goin' on here?' He said, 'I don't blame you; one wheel is missing.' When I got the right pair, I was goin' around like a son-of a-gun. Sometimes you take a partner, and I asked your motha to skate wit me. That's how we met."

They married when she was eighteen at a time within a Catholic culture when girls were expected to grow up, get married, and have lots of babies—two generations worth for Dad and Ma. They had Andy when she was nineteen and Dorothea a year after that and Jackie about a year after Dorothea. Curiously, Ma had Michael about fourteen years after Jackie, then me a little over a year later. Donnie arrived three years after me. Giving birth to six children in the same exact order today would have driven me mad, too. Ma managed working on the floor of a printing company until I was born. Her emotional upheaval began, Dorothea noticed, after Donnie came along.

As road lines blurred by, I thought back to my pregnancies and remembered learning about postpartum depression, a mood disorder sometimes developing in women following childbirth. Donnie was three when Ma committed suicide. Chances of developing postpartum depression increase if the mother suffers from sleep deprivation. Having six children, three under nine years old, and Dad's billing to manage, she likely wasn't resting enough. We can check that box. Another risk factor is having a child with special needs. Check the box. A lack of strong emotional support from a spouse or partner, family, or friends. Dad was out a lot. Her adult children were moving on with their lives. We were often alone with her at night. Check the box. Patients experiencing postpartum depression often feel intense sadness and anxiety. Check the box. Without treatment it can lead to suicide. Check.

That parenthetical "mentally deranged" on Ma's death certificate catches up with me further down the road. As if anyone reading such a death certificate wouldn't understand from its details that Ma dwelled in a dark place. "Mentally deranged"—it's dismissive. Why bother determining why a loving mother and devoted wife would go down into her basement, create a noose from electrical cord, step onto a chair, tie that cord over a wooden beam, place her head into that noose and step off that chair. It's as if that medical examiner thought to himself, "Let's just dub her mentally deranged and move on."

My memories of Ma come irrevocably joined with *how* she died. It took decades for me to do so, but now not a day passes when I don't think of her or her death in some way. It's always *THERE*.

As dark as my days grew in the years following Henry's goodbye, doing myself in never emerged as an option. The pain seemed unbearable at times yet on the scale of human emotional suffering, I hadn't descended all the way down. How far down does it go? I'm not sure, but it's scary to consider that Ma's pain drove her all that way down.

In those final seconds, was her breath immediately extinguished? Did she grab at the cord, trying to loosen it from her neck and kick her feet, desperately trying to find the chair below, thinking it all a bad idea?

I pass signs for Marlborough, Massachusetts—I have about twenty-five minutes left on the road. I remind myself I should read suicide books piling up on my bookshelf—*Silent Grief: Living in the Wake of Suicide*; *No Time to Say Goodbye: Surviving the Suicide of a Loved One*; *Night Falls Fast*; *Suicide-The Tragedy of Hopelessness*. I purchased each holding hope of greater insight and understanding—and each just waits there on my bookshelf. I've had both a desire and an aversion to reading them. The one grief book I did manage to read leapt off the shelf at me more than twenty years ago. I consumed Hope Edelman's *Motherless Daughters*. As I re-read parts of it now, it shocks me to discover that I didn't recognize when I bought the book how much I was still grieving the loss of Ma. That even after reading it, I didn't recognize some warning signals Edelman mentions.

"...But the child who faces continuing difficulties—a father who can't stop grieving, a stepmother who rejects her, an unstable home life—can end up a long way from the point where she once began."

You can say that again, Ms. Edelman!

When I first purchased Edelman's book, I felt ashamed for indulging too much in my own self-pity. Like, well, "I should be over this by now." I didn't know how far I had to go—even then, twenty-five years after my mother died.

I jumped on the exit to the Mass Pike, heading west.

I've heard it's people who make places special. I wonder then, how pilgrimages like ones to my childhood home can elicit such powerful memories even while Ma is no longer there. I think perhaps like Pauline's returning to her childhood home, these visits to mine provide an architecture to rouse my memory. I may feel this way or that way again. I may even pretend for a moment I am back, saying "what if," and considering all possible outcomes that could have been, but having mature insight to answer myself in ways I couldn't all those years ago.

The beauty of this space since losing Ma is that it has sharpened my comprehension yet softened my perspective. History is a kind and loving teacher. Time has been a blessing. I took the exit for Interstate 146 and traveled the last two backroads. Almost home.

Chapter 15

As I walked into my Whitinsville house, it embraced me like my childhood home did before we lost Ma. Vintage homes can do that. They capture our comings and goings in their wear and imperfections— some obvious, some sealed in paint and renovations and the grass that grows over our paths and our troubles. Our stories are no less there. Some believe that we leave energy on everything we touch. That items hold this energy. And that we all carry some ability to sense an object's past by touching it. Over the years, boards of old houses warp, loosen, and creak under our passions—our love, hate, fears, and secrets, so many secrets. Stories likely live in those boards, time capsules waiting to break open.

My childhood house is like an estranged family member. We still love each other but got separated by a tragedy that weakened our bond. My vintage home and I were like a couple who stays up all night just talking because they're so into each other. I adored that place like a good husband. Like any spouse, though, the place had its imperfections, and often I'd have rather not known what they were.

• • •

Punch List Item #3 – Find out why's it's always breezy inside.

Feeling a constant draft inside, I figured I'd better see about getting a home energy assessment. Massachusetts Electric Company sent an energy specialist who tested my heating system and hot water. This young handsome man examined my basement, trudged along the parameter of my home, and crawled across my attic.

When he came back in, he said, "This house breathes well."

I kind of thought that myself, albeit for different reasons. It came as no surprise my home's greatest problem was a lack of insulation. The good news? It qualified for state funding and tax breaks under an energy-efficient home improvement law. My decision seemed a no brainer.

The day insulation contractors came, I arranged working from home and toiled away in my front office. Getting insulation into that older home entailed removing about every fourth piece of siding on the outside and punching a row of holes into the wood underneath, each about the diameter of a hockey puck. Next, workers placed a hose from a truck parked in the street into each hole. The machine blew in a recycled newspaper "cellulose." Once done, they plugged up those hockey puck holes and nailed the exterior siding back on.

It sounded like someone vacuumed my entire house from outside in. The noise interrupted my concentration, but I eventually managed to block it out until Midnight roused. I glanced up. A guy in chalky dust stood before me. He spoke the words no homeowner wants to hear from someone working on their place.

"Can you come out here for a second? I have something to show you."

"Sure."

I scooped up Midnight and followed him outside.

He pointed to a hole in the second story woodwork the size of a windshield, exposing the back of my son's bedroom wall. "When we took those boards off, there was nothing underneath. It looks like it was eaten away. Most likely carpenter ants. They're gone now. That will need fixing before we can put siding back up."

Cuddling Midnight a little closer, I stared up at that gaping hole and felt my chest tighten. "How much will that cost?" I asked.

"I don't know," he said. "We don't do that kind of work. We can recommend someone though. I just wanted to show you. We'll cover it with plastic for now. You'll want to repair it as soon as possible."

"Okay," I said.

I returned to my desk and couldn't concentrate, this time due to financial worry.

I chided myself for allowing contractors to dismantle this antique. "Of course they'd find something wrong," I thought. "We could have gone years not knowing—not caring—what was or wasn't under those boards!"

Why did I feel like a robot someone forgot to program for dealing with this sort of thing? I missed Henry. He could fix anything. He even once installed his own septic system. When the brakes on my car went, he met me at a Massachusetts Turnpike breakdown lane, carrying a bag of tools. Repaired it on the spot.

My depression seemed like that empty space under those boards. Everything appeared fine outside until someone got close enough to remove the layers. I had to figure out this hole in the house on my own. What did I do? Forget about it for a while.

• • •

Despite its disrepair, there remained something comforting about living in my vintage house. Pauline's pilgrimage the year earlier lasted perhaps just thirty minutes. Still, once she led me through the door to my home's past, I never returned. Whenever I saw the hidey-hole, I remembered her family's prudence. Outside, I imagined her mother's gardens. I thought about conversions of this wall and of that one as I walked by them. Her Dutch heritage, and her father's working at Whitin mill and learning to speak English by reading a Bible. How does someone learn English by reading the Bible, anyway? What good fortune to be home that day she visited! To learn some of the stories and the secrets contained within those boards. I had to remember everything she shared with me. To know more about the house and her family's era there.

Having Henry gone for more than two years by 2006 and no other men in sight (although that would change soon enough), I spent my boys' weekends with their dad satiating my curiosity about my house and our local history.

I read online about my town's past until my butt hurt and my coffee soured. Explored books on immigration, the Whitin mill, American economy, and capitalism way back when. Tracked down and spoke to Osterman family descendants and those of Dutch immigrants. Listened to neighbors and local contractors who worked on my house. Then to get a sense of the era, I called a history professor about life then and now. I spent a few afternoons in the Whitinsville Social Library History Room. This digging filled a void left by the reporter job I still missed.

The Dutch migration to Whitinsville did not begin due to fear of religious persecution. It did not start with war or famine. It had nothing to do with jobs or industry—at least not for starters.

It had to do with cows.

In the mid-1880s, Jan Bosma accompanied some Holstein-Friesian cattle, the black and white ones, ordered by Mrs. John C. Whitin, the mill owner's widow. She'd ordered them, to replace some Jersey cows, the brown ones, lost to tuberculosis. Upon arrival to Whitinsville, Jan wrote home to his friends and family saying he'd found "a land of opportunity" here.

Not long afterwards, his sister and her husband came. Then his brother-in-law's brother, *his* wife, and five children came. They were all followed by people named Rienstra and Plantinga and Glashouwer and Werkman and Feenstra and Kooistra. These remain names on local mailboxes, on business signs, and in newspaper articles still today.

Depression tagged along on every exploration, like a sick child who clung to her mother. Having too many responsibilities to sulk in bed all day, I trudged on, working and caring for the boys. Without a trigger it seemed, pain seeped up from my chest and lodged in my throat. Other times, that ache in my throat grew so much that it spread back down into my chest. My depression hijacked any reason to account for its livelihood—financial struggles, relationship issues, work, motherhood.

Back at work, my phone lit up showing an unfamiliar number.

"Hello?" I answered. "Mary, I hate bothering you at work. It's your neighbor, Mary Army," she said.

"Hi Mary. Are you okay?" I asked.

"Yes, but I feel terrible," she said, panicked. "I just yelled at your son, Geoffrey."

"What happened?" I asked.

"He was skateboarding on your garage roof. I was afraid he'd fall off," she said.

"Did he get down?" I yelled into the phone.

"Yes, but I still feel terrible," she said.

"Well, thank you. I'm glad you yelled at him. I'll call him right now to make sure he doesn't do it again."

Here, this neighbor acted kind and caring, didn't yell at my children like the Wall Banger and her spouse. I told myself if I were home, maybe my little daredevil would have thought twice before attempting such a feat. At least he didn't fall and *split his head open.*

Greg spent hours throwing a baseball against a backyard pitch-back net alone instead of with me or Brian. I felt guilty about that, too. He missed catches every now and then and ran into our woods to fetch his ball.

"Mom, I think I've got poison ivy on my legs," he'd say.

"Let me see. Yikes, let's go into the bathroom and take care of that," I'd reply.

Then both of us sat on one side of the old tub, my legs outside, his inside. I ran water over them. Scrubbed his legs using poison ivy wash, timing the treatment for five minutes—following package instructions. Dried them and spread anti-itch cream on them.

At night once the boys settled into their beds, I returned to my research. Worked during the day. Spent downtime at the library, with a local history book, or hunched over my computer.

By the time Mr. Osterman built my house in 1923, about a thousand Dutch families lived in Whitinsville. They were known for their faith, frugality, cleanliness, and discipline. Many came, worked at Whitin for just a few years, then started dairy farms and other businesses. Many who continued working at mills operated farms before and after hours. They created a community renowned for its virtues, well known to descendants and others still there today.

To deepen my understanding, I attended a coffee conversation hour at Pleasant Street Christian Reformed Church, in Whitinsville, the parish the Ostermans attended. Descendants of early Dutch settlers took turns sharing their stories with me that day.

"Back then, Dutch people shunned American influences," said an older gentleman.

"They kept to themselves," a woman said.

Another said, "They established their own church and private school. Dancing, and movies, and amusements, even Sunday newspapers remained forbidden entertainments."

"In those days we had early Sunday morning church services, followed by refreshments at friends' houses and time at home to rest afterward," explained another man. "On Sunday evening, we headed back to church again!"

The church pastor delivered morning services in English, evening services, in Dutch. Most families attended both.

"My father told me that once a man caught a woman in his pew seat. So he sat on her lap, and not in a friendly, sort of way," said the woman.

Those usual seats helped children coming back from religious education to pinpoint and join their parents. I suppose, too, that families easily spotted in their usual pews sent a signal to the pastor and parishioners that they did indeed come to church that day.

In Dutch homes, families kept Bibles in or near kitchens because at dinnertime they read scripture at the table. This remained true for some of the parishioners I spoke with. Having a Dutch Bible or knowing its verses in Dutch beforehand and comparing them to English versions could help a person learn the language. Children also helped their parents decipher words. In Mr. Osterman's case, I'll bet Mrs. Osterman, an American who grew up in a neighboring town, may have helped her husband with words and phrases.

Following my coffee hour with parishioners, they gave me a tour of the church, pointing out where the Ostermans had sat—up front, to the lectern's right side in that small simple sanctuary. Settling for a moment into their pew, I gazed up and saw the grand sanctuary and stained-glass windows of Saint Michael's Catholic Church where, as a child, I prayed kneeling beside Auntie Sister, Ma's sister. Her name was Madeline. We kids always called her Auntie Sister because she was a nun. She wore long layers of white robes and a black veil covering her hair and ears and draping way down her back. This ensemble created her *habit*. Black rosary beads hung at her waist. Her black shoes peeped out from under robes.

Sitting in the Ostermans' pew, I remembered how as a little girl, I felt privileged alongside Auntie Sister at church. I could walk behind her right up into the sanctuary as if we were royalty. I recalled the safety of her hugs, inside those layers of her robes.

Sometimes Ma left me for an afternoon at the convent with Auntie Sister who taught elementary school. Seated in the last row of her classroom, I struggled to complete worksheets her older students whizzed through. After school, she and I knelt at the church altar and said our prayers, then joined other nuns at the convent where I helped Auntie Sister do chores. There were rows and rows of washing machines and dryers in that convent cellar where those layers and layers of robes were laundered. She leaned into washing machines and hand over hand, like a fisherman hoisting his net from the sea, yanked out a large ball of tangled white hosiery.

"Oh, it's that little man in the washing machine again," she said. "He goes in there and tangles up all our stockings."

Together, we worked out the thick knots and she reached up on her tippy toes to sling those hose over a clothesline extending the length of the big cellar.

An ordinary day became a holiday whenever Auntie Sister visited us. We honored her as our family monarch. Ma spread out a linen tablecloth and served tea in painted bone china teacups. Dad came home from work early and drank homemade iced tea from a tall glass adorned by a wedge of lemon hanging on its rim—instead of his usual beer. No one swore while Auntie Sister visited. Dad even turned down his police scanner in her presence.

Auntie Sister smiled and hugged me into her robes. She gave me packages wrapped in white tissue paper and pink, yellow, or light blue satin ribbons. I opened them to find a set of pastel crayons, scented soaps, hand-embroidered hankies, pretty note paper, or little prayer books. These were gifts given to her that she sacrificed, re-gifting them to me.

Auntie Sister placed Donnie on her lap.

"Pat-a-cake, pat-a-cake, baker's man..." she'd say in rap-rhythm rhyme as she clapped Donnie's hands together. He'd chuckle. I'd frown. I wanted Auntie Sister all to myself. Sensing my sadness, she'd catch my eye and say, "Mary Gayle, do you know your brother, Donnie, is very special?"

"I don't see anything special about him," I'd say in a pouty voice, just as I'd say to Ma whenever she said Donnie was *special*.

Auntie Sister thought this sounded hilarious and quoted me many times later. It took years for me to understand why this was so funny. During our goodbyes, Auntie Sister whispered in my ear, "Do you know you can be anything you want to be when you grow up, even the president?"

After Ma died, I didn't see Auntie Sister quite as often. When she did visit, we didn't mention Ma, but by the way water filled her eyes upon seeing us kids, I knew she was thinking of Ma.

I rose from the bench and thanked the parishioners for their hospitality and for their stories.

While my sense of spirituality remains private these days, I see now how a greater communal experience like the Ostermans' provided a sense of belonging. Dutch settlers and those like them attended church to be closer to God *and each other*. Perhaps that's where God lives—in those intangible bonds that unite us and in that sense of *possibility* we call hope.

Chapter 16

Like the Ostermans surely had over their lifetime in that house, we also endured our share of economic crises there, too. During our first several years there, the United States economy shifted for worsening times. As a single mother with loose spending habits, I lived on the edge of a personal financial meltdown. The Great Recession seemed to impact me sooner than most people—canary in coalmine style. Long before "subprime mortgage" earned its keep as a household term, everything, particularly heating oil, became more difficult to pay for. I felt myself slipping further behind. Working as hard as ever, I swam toward a dock floating farther away instead of closer. Depending on a paycheck coming every week as much as a sun rising every morning, I didn't know corporate leaders were discussing a cost benefit analysis for my dismissal. Meanwhile my beloved house required constant renovations.

· · ·

Punch List Item #4 – Fix gaping hole in siding.

Turns out I couldn't forget about the hole in the house. Visions of Greg, Geoff, or their friends fooling around inside and falling against and through that bedroom wall and down to the patio below haunted me. To fix the problem, I interviewed about three contractors. I chose Roger for two reasons: One, he specialized in old houses and two, he appreciated my place.

"In those days, they knew how to put houses together," he said. "Now they just slap 'em up using cheap materials."

Working years in sun and wind leathered Roger's face. He explained necessary repairs in such detail, it seemed he was training me, as if he expected me to grab a hammer and start helping.

"See those nails?" He put his index finger on a spot of rust seeping from an old nail head on the siding. He held his finger there and said, "That's rusted because they didn't use galvanized nails. I always use galvanized nails," he said, as he gave me a serious ten-second stare. Pressing his finger into the rusted nail again and shaking his head in disgust, he said, "I would never do that."

To fix the hole in my house, he installed new wood and insulation inside and new siding outside. The restored section had a smooth finish. The remaining siding still looked like new nail polish applied over a chipped undercoat. Every day, I'd rub my hand over that old siding and imagine a prouder house with all new boards. Roger estimated about fifteen- to twenty-grand for the entire house—a kind of money I didn't have back then, at least not all at once.

"You don't have to do it all at once," he said. "You can do just one side at a time and pay me for just what we do every year."

Counting all its various angles, the house had roughly twenty sides, albeit some areas measured just a few feet wide. Every year for about seven or so, Roger replaced just one to three sides at once.

When he finished the entire house, I shook my head, considering my initial fear over a few rotten boards on the outside of my house. After all, those boards had been there for decades and might have held up for decades longer. I guess most fears are hallucinations. Problems can be patient. Whenever big repairs couldn't be done, there was usually an interim remedy. Getting better takes time. That old house and me—we made progress and never let each other completely down.

• • •

My depression hijacked the idea that to overcome sadness, I needed a man in my life again. I began fitting in dates whenever I could—back to the online numbers game: I met a man who often cancelled dates, calling "from the airport." A guy who explained how he'd had a Wiccan witch cast a spell on a former girlfriend.

"It was nothing bad," he said. "I just wanted her to stop focusing on me."

A guy who on our first and only date complained of a cluster headache, went to a men's room, and never returned. At least a half-dozen others didn't go well for one reason or another before I met Dennis on eHarmony. It was September 2006.

I was about forty-six. He was about forty-nine. A rougher version of George Clooney, he spoke in a raspy voice and an academic accent. Where from, I couldn't tell. It wasn't an ethnic accent, but a *learned* accent, where he accentuated and held last syllables of most words. It seemed in context, though, seeing he had a Mercedes to go with it. Was it a Mercedes C Class or E Class? I never noticed.

This handsome guy with a head full of salt and peppers loved concerts and theater and dining out and weekends in Manhattan. He lived in a McMansion-style home in a swanky little Connecticut town along the Long Island Sound—not a man I'd run into at my local Shaw's Supermarket in Whitinsville.

We enjoyed a first date at WaterFire. My idea. An artsy event in Providence, Rhode Island, fires crackled inside hundreds of black caldrons anchored in a straight line down the middle of the city's canals. A campfire aroma and "world" music—like yoga music—piped in through speakers filled the city. Mobs of people migrated to cobblestone walkways along the canal. We sat on the edge with our feet dangling over water, our eyes worshipping the flames.

Black boats carrying an abundance of wood crept across waterways all night. Fire starters, wearing black from head-to-toe, traveled in these boats to ignite and feed the flames. As a boat crawled past a caldron, crew onboard leaned over and each placed a log into the fire. A synchronized dance. Every addition of wood forced a barrage of sparks high into our black sky. As fire tenders ignited wood in the first caldrons, people cheered. Fire starters, though, remained stoic, blending into night. No waving. No yelling from boats.

We talked about him. About me. About what happened to our marriages. He asked about my parents. I explained that Dad died at eighty-one and Ma much earlier.

"Oh, I'm sorry to hear that. Was she sick?" he asked.

"She died tragically," I said. "Maybe I'll tell you about it someday, but not tonight." That's always my initial response to those who don't know me well. I'm always worried people will jump to judging me. Analyze the impact of the tragedy on me. How it *affected* me. How it *damaged* me. Only after I've gained someone's trust can I share more details. I've made mistakes in this. I once responded to a young, trusted co-worker who asked how Ma died and immediately regretted my words.

"It's terrible so brace yourself," I warned. "But just know that I'm okay now. I've had time to process it. My mother committed suicide by hanging herself in our basement."

My co-worker's response was nothing. She said nothing. That's when I knew it was too much information for her. Once I said it, I could not un-say it. Could not hope she might forget about it. She will never forget about it. As an adult, I now understand better my family's silence. With our secret intact, we could continue looking okay on the outside.

Dennis asked if Dad ever remarried and I told him he did, trying to explain things in a way that didn't make my childhood sound like the *Jerry Springer* special it was. That's the thing with a crazy family. You always have explaining to do—or to dance around.

Dennis met all my list's criteria—and more. We had differences, though. He was well off, residing in his five-thousand-square-foot colonial near the shore. I was broke. He traveled to China several times a year. I traveled daily traffic-gnarled commutes along Interstate 146, then a maze of backroads afterwards to retrieve the boys. He had raised stepchildren who, at that time, attended high school and college. Saw them only occasionally but loved them as his own. For my boys, I considered daily where they were every minute, what they were eating, what they were wearing, how they felt, and who they were with. Drove them hither and thither. Made their meals, picked up after them, attended to their schoolwork, and too many other necessities to mention. He worked from home pretty much whenever he felt like it. I toiled within a four-by six-foot cubicle every day whether I felt like it or not. He could afford meals out, theater, and concerts. I couldn't. He was punctual. I was late.

With a house and a man, my depression convinced me a lack of money accounted for my sadness. Maybe my mind contrived my new obsession from an extreme difference between my and Dennis's finances. While working in Providence, I'd take lunchtime walks from Empire Street, up Westminster, then College Hill, and past RISDI, which everyone pronounces as *risdy*. (It stands for *Rhode Island School of Design*.) Then I'd head up toward the gates of Brown University, back down the hill, taking Waterman this time, over onto Westminster, and onto Empire. Powered on worry, my mind toiled over my budget spreadsheets the whole way.

Figuring logic up Westminster, "Pay heating bill this month, send plumber forty-five dollars a week until that six-hundred-dollar bill is paid." I memorized my checkbook balance. Hiking up College Hill, I considered expenses rushing toward me to diminish it.

Onto Waterman, I wondered, "Are there investment strategies, a second job, a new job, cuts to my budget? Could we grow our own food like the Ostermans probably did?" Back on Westminster, I puzzled over what I'd do when my five-year adjustable-rate mortgage expired.

I wondered if I could earn a promotion while I didn't know company executives would soon plan to fire me.

Whenever my checking account went to pennies, I used credit cards like tickets. I worked a little longer every day, raced highways and backroads to pick up my boys. Again, always late. We often didn't sit down to eat until past seven. News of the mortgage crisis streamed morning and evening news, providing a vocabulary for my financial misery. Subprime mortgage. Recession. Great Recession.

By this time, both boys decided they didn't like living in our vintage home anymore. As soon as their infatuation with the yard and their new bedrooms wore off, their loathing began. "I hate being stuck on a hill!" Geoff protested.

"Why can't we sell this house and go back to our old neighborhood?" Greg said.

Even if I could have sold our house then, I couldn't risk it. Not during a recession. While the boys stormed over their inconvenient locations, too far to walk to friends' homes. I listened, seeing what they couldn't: their independence on the horizon.

Living in a place others inhabited before us, comparisons between their lives then and ours surfaced all around. So many relics. Those workbenches, that hidey-hole, small closets, cupboards, and ancient arches, as well as the worn doorknobs, hinges, and other hardware Mr. Osterman saved and were still in his basement bins. Unlike how my priors saved money under floorboards, I treated my checking account like a personal Ponzi scheme, with necessities purchased the week before jeopardizing my ability to acquire them the next.

My priors' financial picture remained of course a mystery. I never found statements or tried researching their various expenses. However, I did know this much: There were no credit cards in the 1940s. If you wanted something, you saved up for it first. People held mortgages and paid outright for other assets. Their down payments on homes were larger than ours.

There were no malls, no drive-thrus, or ATM machines. Most families got by on one income. From what I heard, the Ostermans had a somewhat self-sustaining lifestyle. Eggs from their chickens, milk from their cow, and vegetables from their garden—they probably spent relatively a lot less on food than I do. Because Mr. Osterman built his house and repaired it himself, he and his wife likely spent a lot less on mortgage and fix ups than I do. Pauline said she and her parents lived in a tiny four-room house on the property while her dad built their home. They may not have had a mortgage.

Dutch people were frugal. "The Dutch farmers got more from an acre and more from a cow than any other farmer in Worcester County. How? Lime and manure, plowing, new seed, top dressing," wrote Louis Lyons in a 1926 article in *The Boston Globe*, "*1,000 Dutch Families in the Bay State Show Us How to Use Our Land.*" While the Ostermans were probably not well off back then, it seems they lived a good life well within their means.

Relying on store-bought stuff, my "necessities" included goods that didn't exist during their day, like a smartphone and computer and internet access and Starbucks grande decaf mocha Americanos, "firming" moisturizer, French manicures, and pedicures. The Ostermans probably could have eaten for a year on my monthly spending for these items.

I purchased my beloved home in 2004 amid a home-buying frenzy. Yes, it was old. Yes, it required a constant diet of repairs. But it was a 2,100 square-foot, solid gem on an acre-plus lot. My bank packed on a second mortgage.

"There you go sweetheart," it conveyed. "We're so happy for you."

My monthly mortgage payments were about $2,382. This amount included a second mortgage I took out when I purchased the place because the maximum amount on the first one didn't suffice. This sort of thing—lending such a whopping amount to a single person earning just $74,000 a year, nearly half of which came from child support ending within less than ten years—fueled the eventual financial market's collapse. "This sort of thing" wasn't done back in the Ostermans' day.

Like many of my friends and family members, I danced on the precipice of bankruptcy. But by the grace of a consumer society, I still managed soaking my feet in warm water Saturday mornings while sipping gourmet coffee and reading a good book as a spa technician scrubbed and massaged my toes.

Amid all this, my look back at the house and its history began taking on a new meaning. This vintage place started preaching to me each day about what had been and why. Stone walls, patios, and woodwork *in this modest home* spoke of its priors' pride and creativity. Smaller rooms were easier to heat. Less closet space meant fewer clothes. Two magnificent workbenches not only told that repairs and fix ups were done by owners, but that perhaps there came some joy in doing them. Leftover broken light fixtures and scraps of wood and single windowpanes were saved for reuse. Hand waxed floors meant, sure, better technology didn't exist, but that these people took care of what they had. A mill at the bottom of the road conveyed work waited nearby. Cash stowed in a hidey-hole promised money for later.

Fast forward to my life. I gardened, cleaned a little, and changed batteries and light bulbs, maybe weed whacked if I could get my beast working. That's about it. Most of my time there, I drove about fifty miles a day into cities where crops of tall buildings looked like behemoth graveyards on my ride in. While I worked at a desk there, no one managed things at home. During summers and after-school hours, I pieced for the boys a mosaic of summer camps and school programs, playdates, and once they became old enough, time home alone. Even though I love working, leaving them each day broke my heart. I admit, I've always been a spender, but let's face it, while managing a home and a couple of kids, a modest income doesn't stretch far.

Rummaging through my assumptions about families still intact, I craved a frame of reference. What did it take? How was it done? I found myself praising my house's priors—for their wisdom in faith and community and frugality and family values—all virtues they *constructed* to survive in this foreign place.

For all our differences, my priors and I had something in common. Surviving a choppy childhood and trying to cope through early divorce, I dwelled in a foreign place, too.

Chapter 17

There stood Dennis, so kind and generous, taking me to concerts and theater and dinners. He sent actual notes though the actual mail, too.

"Wish I may, wish I might..."

The guy framed pictures of us together. Created a scrapbook chronicling our relationship. We dropped Greg and his friend, Nick, off at a movie theater one night in 2007.

"Meet me at the trunk," he said to the boys.

At the trunk, he handed each of them a jumbo Charleston Chew. They thanked him, stuffed the contraband under their sweatshirts, and dashed into the theater giggling.

He was "a top-shelf guy," a term he used for men he respected. While I so appreciated all he did, I didn't show it. I feared showing it. To make another man think I wanted him to "blend." While most other women may have gone to extremes to please a man of his character, I felt satiated by my own vintage place, to learn about it and from it, and to keep it for myself. I had fallen in love with a house.

• • •

Punch List Item #5 – Stop indoor tsunami.

Despite Dennis's affluence, he always brought his toolbox with him when he came to visit. Knowing I lived in an older place, he thought it a good contingency.

After spending every other weekend with each other for a long stretch, I needed a break—just to do stuff at home. To give ourselves a chance to catch up, we agreed on skipping one of our usual weekends together. On our Saturday off, I wore yoga pants, a sleeveless shirt, no makeup, my hair thrown in a careless ponytail. Bare feet. Facing my bow window vacuuming cobwebs overhead, I thought I imagined the sight when his car crawled up my driveway. Split between running to the bathroom for makeup or my bedroom for better clothes, I figured I had time for neither. Threw my hands up and surrendered to the door. Midnight made it there first.

"Hey, I thought we were taking a break this weekend," I said, hugging him.

"I know, but I thought I'd come and power wash your house for you," he said.

"Yeah, right," I thought. "You drive two and half hours just to power wash my house?" "Okay," I said. "That would be great. Come in and let me change."

"No, you look great," he said. "Don't let me stop what you're doing. Just tell me where your water spigot is."

Midnight slid onto the floor and tried to settle back into her nap as I went back to sucking up cobwebs while Dennis hooked up his power washer to our outdoor water. With the vacuum moaning, I didn't hear our door fly back open. Dennis rushed into the kitchen from outside. Midnight shot after him. I shut off the noise.

"Hey, what's up?" I said.

"Where's the shut-off valve for your spigot?" he asked.

"In the basement. Why? What's wrong?" I said.

"We need to shut it off," he said.

We raced downstairs. Midnight stood watch from atop. A torrent of water poured into my cellar from an inside connection to the outdoor spigot. Scrambling about, we found the lever and stopped the flood. He appeared worried. I, pissed. He showed up when I craved solitude and unleashed a tsunami into my basement.

"I'll call my plumber and tell him it's an emergency," I said.

"No, I can fix it," he said.

"You can?" I said.

"Yes, where's your hardware store?" he asked.

Within an hour, he replaced the broken fixture and pipe, installing a stronger handle on the outside. My spigot broke because I forgot to shut off an outdoor water line in late fall. During some frigid hour the previous winter, water froze inside that little copper pipe, expanding and cracking it open. As Dennis turned the handle outside, water exploded through the inside portion of the compromised pipe. I felt fortunate it happened while he was there. He encroached on my boundary that day and left me better off.

. . .

On a whim that summer, Dennis and I explored outside the Whitin mill complex. Set against the Mumford River waterfall, the building sprawls out like a cat in a sunny window, its bricks and windows and bricks and windows as far as sight will stretch. We parked in an empty lot nearby and strolled into the factory yard. The water crashed over that waterfall.

"Wow. I love old factories like this," he said. "Look at details in the architecture."

We observed the medieval tower built into the mill's side.

"I could just imagine Rapunzel letting down her hair from that window," I said, pointing up at an arched window. I wondered which part of Whitin mill Mr. Osterman may have worked in. We walked under the building's overpass into a sort of tunnel-like area under one of its main floors. While Dennis and I courted, I abandoned my research, and it tugged at me that day, like missing Sunday Mass weighs on a devout Catholic.

"This must have been something in its heyday," Dennis said.

That remained one of our better summer days in Whitinsville. As much as I loved that town, it wasn't the place to be on hot summer days for someone who owned a home by the sea. Staying in Whitinsville with me, Dennis yearned for his home by the ocean. I preferred weekends in Whitinsville near my boys, rather than at his beach community. My constant tardiness got on his nerves. Without children of his own, he couldn't imagine last-minute laundry, unanticipated rides to and pickups from friends' houses, or my throwing fresh sheets on everyone's beds before leaving for weekends away.

Deep down, though, I felt afraid. Henry awakened in me the complexity of placing children in the middle. I didn't want to blend after all. What would a second marriage in shambles look like for me and my boys? They had been through enough as children of divorce. Best I could do was try keeping things afloat between just me and the kids while they were young. Maybe I didn't need a man to make my house a home after all. I wanted to go slowly. However, to Dennis, I slacked on relationship building. In a way he was right. With the boys, the house, and work, it became hard finding energy for the wardrobe and the manicures and the time a man like that expected from a girl like me.

Ending it during a summer evening walk that year, I regretted my decision by the time I got home. Called him. Sent him long, sappy emails. Wrote letters. Even considered manipulating my way back into his heart by writing a letter from Midnight to his two cats. Never sent that one. In September 2007, following our breakup, I drove two and half hours to his place, just to bring him orange juice. After all, he had a cold. He thanked me, forcing a smile, took the juice and closed his door. Driving out of his town, my phone lit up twice showing his name. Each time I answered, he hung up—as if his brain and heart fought a tug-of-war. Each time he hung up, I hit his number to call him back. His brain prevailed. No answer.

I didn't want to become his *Fool Calling*, so I just gave up. We were all going down—our relationship, the economy, my home's value. I braced myself, thinking my depression would knock me to the ground and leave me crawling and when I got up, staggering. However, this new letdown hardly registered on my disappointment scale. While I felt sad, I didn't go *all that way* back down—to that lowest low I'd fallen after Henry left.

I can't say how or pinpoint when. It seemed about then that I stopped feeling ridiculed and inadequate. Financial numbers stopped firing off in my head. Pains in my chest vanished. Laughter came easily. Even though I was alone, I wasn't lonely. Woke up one day and discovered my depression gone. For days afterward, my brain ran through its daily checklist: Throat? No lump. Chest? No pain. Head? No worry. It felt like awaking after weeks and weeks with a cold to realize I could breathe through my nose again. Refreshing.

Immersing back into my research felt good. For the next couple of years, I continued working, caring for things at home, and exploring my house's history as often as I could.

I studied the Whitin mill that Dennis and I toured on that hot summer day. The best place for learning about this mill—located just two miles away from the house—is by traveling forty miles east to Harvard Business School's Baker Library in Cambridge, which houses most mill archives. Billing and order statements, payroll records, journals, income tax statements, thousands of letters, and too many other artifacts to list—all catalogued by topic in alphanumeric order.

I coerced Geoff into serving as my research assistant. It's a bit intimidating, approaching steps toward the white Baker Library building's six columns. We opened its heavy door and wandered down a wide corridor, not sure which way to turn. We arrived at a room of high ceilings stretching above rows of long tables. Desk lamps on those tables tossed a quaint glow over the room. Ecclesiastical. A curator signed us in, assigned a locker for our jackets and my purse. She explained she'd bring us one archive box at a time upon our request.

"Before taking a photo of a document, please insert this paper at the bottom," she said.

About the size of a mailing label, it said, "Property of the Baker Library."

Geoff and I sat at a long table and dug into the first box. Geoff squinted, holding a piece of paper.

"Exactly, what are we looking for, Mom?" he asked.

"Any clues about what life was like for immigrants who came to Whitin mill in the eighteen- and nineteen-hundreds, how much they were paid, what kind of work they did, anything about working conditions."

The boxes contained *original* handwritten documents—in calligraphy detailing Whitin mill's transactions, work orders, and sales.

"Mom I can't read this fancy handwriting," Geoff said.

Looking a bit frustrated, my boy passed me a paper.

"Look at it," he said.

"No computers back then, honey," I said. "Keep trying. You'll get used to it."

He raised his eyebrows and picked out another paper from the box, read it briefly, then pulled out another and another.

"Look at this." He passed me an original letter written early during the Civil War from a southern factory trying to collaborate with the Whitins on getting machinery from Whitinsville to Alabama by sea through Havana, knowing they wouldn't make it over land borders from north to south.

April 24th, 1861

The present unfortunate state of affairs renders us very uneasy about our machinery. We want the machinery very bad. I have the money ready in Gold to pay for same, but do not know how to arrange for its shipment. Would like very much to hear from you under the circumstances.

The present state of affairs are entirely unexpected to us and it seems really probable that the North and South will be fighting each other without recourse or regret, and there is no telling where it will end. My proposition to you is for you to make arrangements with some Boston House to ship the machinery all on one Vessel to [Havanna]. We will arrange with any party selected there at [Havanna] to pay the Gold for the machinings at price agreed. Ship all on one vessel and let it be a foreign vessel and there will be no risk. ...

PROPERTY OF THE BAKER LIBRARY

"Our own little Whitinsville mill engulfed in the Civil War," I said. "Take a picture of it."

He slipped the library attribution label at the bottom and snapped it.

I looked away from the paper and saw our country then, in 2010, embroiled in rough times again. Albeit not as horrendous as civil war, the Great Recession idled over us. Across the country, Americans were losing jobs. Smaller workforces meant my company's customers were buying fewer health insurance plans from us. The company estimated losing about a hundred million dollars a year and began restructuring. Soon after arriving each morning, employees were often escorted into unexpected meetings.

A manager addressed us, "So and So is no longer here. I cannot elaborate on circumstances surrounding his departure. If you were working with So and So on a project or have questions, please see Such and Such instead. We will not be filling this position. That's all I have."

Everyone shuffled from the meeting room, exchanging awkward glances and phony smiles. After several of these meetings, I questioned if and when I might become a "So and So."

The papers in the boxes told a different story. During Whitin mill days, mill owners and laborers not only lived near each other, but also shared an intricate mutual reliance extending across their community and affecting their disparate lives—a loyalty now as obsolete as equipment Whitin produced.

The Whitins directed political, social, religious, and even electrical affairs. They edited the Village church pastor's weekly sermon and encouraged workers to vote for the company's preferred politicians. A light fixture outside town hall ran on factory wiring. Shop pipes warmed the town hall and community center where residents today still work out and swim.

The Whitins donated land for the then Whitinsville Hospital and paid for a new high school, which now serves as a town office. They established and financed a semi-pro baseball team and offered residents land for growing fresh vegetables, a crop share program that still provides interested residents a patch of land for growing stuff. A magnificent sprawling space located way off a dirt backroad two miles from my vintage home. A patchwork of fenced square plots, each showcasing the whimsical or practical nature of its keeper. Most have rain barrels rigged in a variety of ways for catching water from storms. Some have neatly sowed rows, and a shovel or hoe resting upright in a corner against a fence. Others are adorned by garden gnomes, bird baths, wind chimes, and pinwheels.

A Whitin workplace policy I found said if the shop lacked work, managers tried to avoid laying off employees with dependents. Instead, if orders declined, the company decreased hours for everyone. Mill owners financed maintenance work and other projects within the village when orders slowed.

We had no such policy at my workplace and soon enough, it became my turn to go. My departure came on a Wednesday in June 2010. A normal day, I grabbed coffee at our company café on the way to my office. Shared small talk with colleagues before settling into work. Logged into my computer and became steeped in a project detailing healthcare reform. I promised to send items to colleagues by week's end. To meet with another employee for a webinar next day. My phone rang.

"Mary, can you please come to my office?" said a voice from Human Resources. "I need to give you an update."

"May I ask what this is about?" I said.

"I'll tell you when you come down," she said.

I knew. I hurried toward her office, thinking how my finances rested against that regular paycheck. I walked in. She closed the door.

"We are eliminating your position, effective immediately," she said. "I need you to sign some papers. Then I must escort you out."

My mind raced to my budget. "What's there? What bills are due this month? How much in my savings account?"

"Is there severance pay?" I asked.

"There isn't," she said.

I don't remember the quarter mile or so walk to my parking lot that day. I got into my car and froze—managing to hold myself together for driving home, avoiding a public meltdown.

During the 1870 Depression when orders ran out, Whitin mill workers built a wall of oversized cobblestones, hewn and fit into place. A six-foot-tall, six-mile-long gray boundary, ribboning fallow fields and surrounding wetlands. The wall still encases ruins of a stone slaughterhouse. Five square windows, cupola, and courtyard. For locals today who know its origin, Whitinsville's ancient Castle Hill Farm symbolizes the meaning of work during hard times. Otherwise underemployed mill workers spent three years clearing land and stacking stones to build that wall. Milk and other dairy foods were produced on the farm and sold at the company store. Castle Hill Farm later brought the cows and their caregivers from Holland, caregivers who encouraged their Dutch friends and relatives, including Mr. Osterman, to come here, too—and build the gambrel I derived so much solace from.

Coming upon the ruins of that stone barn almost made me delusional at first, forgetting for a moment I stood within my own neighborhood. Great Britain, France, Italy, Holland maybe? The reality is stunning. The remnants of this farm are obviously not *in* one of those places, but *of* those places—it arrived through the calloused hands of its immigrant craftsmen.

I recognize, though, factory work meant hard work. Eleven-hour days. Little pay. For forty or fifty years of workers' lives. No paid vacation. For those who received a pension, it wasn't much.

That day I lost my job, I raced home, fired up my laptop, and contacted former colleagues about potential freelance writing projects. I thought about Dad and how he never worked for anyone else most of his life. He opened his towing and car repair shop, put out his sign, and people brought in their worn brakes, loud mufflers, and steamy radiators. Customers and police beckoned Dad to roads all hours of day and night to tow vehicles when those cars were too broken to start or their drivers too drunk to drive.

Within weeks writing projects came *to my shop*. By fall that year, I became self-sufficient, earning nearly twice my prior salary. I guess I built my own stone wall and garage.

Without long commutes over the next several years, I cooked better meals, kept our house cleaner and maybe more organized, and spent more time listening to my boys. I only regret it came later, after Greg started high school and Geoff, college.

Having my own writing business, I've raced from shower to home office, the small half octagon room at the front of the house, attending conference calls, then tearing away at the keyboard, writing health literature. In that little room, I articulated what hundreds of Affordable Care Act provisions meant to patients and doctors. Wrote how researchers can uncover human genome expression patterns pinpointing what makes us sick and better. Deciphered clinical information about a drug for hepatitis and explained how it reduced numbers of nodules on patients' livers. Discovered and articulated the value of physical therapy for cancer survivors.

Perfecting details like these all day in that little room, I still felt like I just came home when walking out into other parts of the house. The place welcomed me that way.

To manage my phobia of work shortage, I chose a date a month away on my calendar every four weeks and in that spot, I wrote: "APPOINTMENT WITH MY FEAR." Then as Fear Day approached, I assessed whether I had a lack of work to worry about. I never did. Work kept coming, and I stopped making appointments with my fear years ago.

My new work life came, too, just as Midnight descended into old age. She began having more accidents inside. Outdoors, she trotted in stutters, breaking her gait in sudden halts as if experiencing mild electric shocks on her journey to our backyard because, I supposed, she couldn't see well. The vet diagnosed her with a nervous condition. Despite drinking copious volumes of water, she couldn't satiate her thirst. She required several trips a day outside to relieve herself and medicines three times a day. She slept most of the time and seldom played. I knew her time was near and dreaded how and when it might happen.

While I brushed my teeth before bed during this time, she began gasping for air. I ran to her dog bed. As she lay there, stretching her neck out, reaching for air, I feared touching her, thinking she might bite me. That's strange I know for this gentle creature who never showed aggression. But in all her seventeen years, I'd never seen her act this way. I stood back. Then she stopped. Stopped gasping. Stopped moving. She left me.

I knelt beside her and patted her, wishing I had done so seconds ago. Even while watching death take her, I didn't know it was happening until it was done. I remembered how earlier that day, I had dipped cotton balls into warm water and eased brown guck from each of her eyes.

My cheeks soaking, I carried her in her dog bed and placed it on my car's front passenger seat. At Foster Hospital for Small Animals, a technician wrapped her in a blanket and gave me a few minutes alone holding her in a room containing only a cold stainless-steel examining table. Cuddling her to my chest, I cried at how life exits a being in a breath. I cried for Rinney's frozen body. I cried for his chains, and for my cold-hearted reaction when he died. I cried at losing Midnight, our furry sidekick. I cried for the end of an era. I just cried.

Chapter 18

I agreed to cremate Midnight. A crematory poured her ashes into a small wooden box, screwed its lid shut, and mailed them to me. I stepped into our basement to find a place for them and decided against keeping her remains down there. I opted instead for a living room cabinet. I went down to the basement only occasionally, perhaps to switch a breaker, check the oil tank gauge, and since the tsunami, shut off water to that outdoor spigot during late fall. Oh, and once, to deal with something nasty.

• • •

Punch List Item #6 – Repair poop pump.

In every love affair, there comes a recognition in discovering the object of my affection has some offensive imperfection. A darker imperfection than all his others. Too often, I discover the problem only after I'm all in.

I reached up, grabbing a few things from a kitchen cupboard and thought, "What's that smell?"

I opened the basement door and took a whiff: It smelled like a port-a-potty. In my affection for my vintage house, that offensive imperfection came in discovering a device known as a "sewage ejection system."

Let me explain.

All of our wastewater traveled to a tall cylinder tank located at the bottom of the basement steps. Whenever its sensor signaled, "full," a powerful pump ejected forty gallons of raw sewage at the velocity of an egg exploding in a microwave through a thick pipe, shooting it eighty yards away into our backyard septic system. Whenever I explained this, people always said, "Yuck," exactly as I did the first time I heard about it. Unfortunately, by then, it had become one of my possessions.

That's why no one else's *Yuck* out accentuated my own. I'm not sure if knowing about this poop tank beforehand would have changed my mind about buying the house. It just diminished some of my enchantment with the place—like the first time you smell your lover's fart.

The day I smelled crap in the basement, I ran down and stood on the bottom step—because terrain beyond was covered in everything that should have dumped into that tank over the last twenty-four hours or so. That's why I ran back upstairs even faster. Fecal matter on a floor will turn a casual Saturday apocalyptic. One-thousand dollars, a new pump, and about five buckets of bleachy water later, everything worked just fine again. Still, I had to walk through life remembering that big barrel full of shit in my basement.

· · ·

Even with lights on, it stayed as gray as a snowless winter down there. The crumbling cement floor remained dirtier than anything I'd ever cleaned. Asbestos-wrapped pipes hung overhead, so I wore a face mask when I went down. I stored nothing of my own in the basement. Dusted with all matter of what falls down from a cellar ceiling over a century, this part of our house memorialized its former craftsman.

As much as I hated our basement, it contained one compelling element: the workbench. This place to rework and rebuild stood at the basement's far end, tucked into its own corner. To get there, I passed boilers, a canning room, and a coal room. Finally, at the basement's opposite end, there it stood. A wooden workbench about the width of a twin bed and length of two. Its coffee brown surface remained sturdy despite all its scars, burns, and gouges. Under one end laid a stack of four drawers—two smaller-width drawers side-by-side and two wider ones below them. Two more drawers sat under its bench-top—one midway down and another toward its far end. Opening these drawers required a series of sticky starts and stops, and patience for enduring my disappointment in discovering them empty. Two shelves hung above the bench, also empty. Light streamed in through cobwebs across the workbench from the dusty window above.

Standing at the bench and turning around, I once examined a stack of about twenty wooden bins from ceiling to floor. I pushed cobwebs away. Exploring what they held inside, I found the bins packed with leftover metal parts, screws, bolts, panes of glass, used hinges and wooden handholds, broken light fixtures, old doorknobs, and metal gadgets I could not name. Mr. Osterman's? I know I should have demanded that the people I purchased my home from take this stuff out before I moved in. To be honest, I was so overwhelmed with buying the house and moving that I overlooked doing so—and I'm kind of glad I did. Besides other relics, these artifacts conveyed a commitment to repairing the house's broken parts.

I claimed another old workbench, one in our garage, for gardening projects. My garage bench stood just as big and at a perfect height for reaching everything. Its wide surface offered enough room for all of my pots and bags of soil, leaving loads of open bench space. A dependable surface, it never budged under the heft of my urns or vibration of my drill for boring drainage holes in pots.

The bench's dark worn surface seemed only enriched by the dirt and mud and dents I contributed. Spending hours out there during warm weather days and nights, I slipped on gloves and grabbed a vintage iron basket. Placed it on my bench beside a bucket of water, a bag of soil, and plants. I noticed an old coffee can nailed to the wall and mounted below it, a well-worn crank pencil sharpener. Rows of hand built wooden cubbies hung on an adjacent wall. Mr. Osterman's?

I dug into some sphagnum moss to line my basket. Having an imagination fueled by discussions with Pauline and others I've talked to, I saw Mr. Osterman tinkering at *his* bench in the basement under his wife's methodic footsteps, moving from refrigerator to counter, to stovetop, as she prepared dinner, and under scampering of his children's feet. He fished something out of his bins.

Dipping moss into water, I pressed the grassy stuff against my basket's sides. I bailed out potting soil from a bag and poured the black dirt into my basket. I imagined Mr. Osterman digging out the heavy, black metal pan from his bins. Did he strip it from a broken appliance? He turned back around and placed that object into his vice grip and fashioned the metal into a smaller pan to collect oil drippings from his car until it could be fixed. I imagined Pauline in her plaid dress and pigtails finding her father at his bench and telling him it's almost dinnertime. Maybe he turned only his head, acknowledged her with eye contact, and didn't speak a word, like Dad did when I interrupted him at work. Pauline ran back upstairs and reported she dispatched her mother's message.

I banged a potted pink petunia upside-down against my opposite palm, dislodged it, tore off its tangled roots, and set it into soil. Gazing up, I read a sign on the garage wall: "One Operator at a Time." Mr. Osterman's?

There surely must have been a day when he tightened lids on containers of oils and lubricants I found inside his bins—*an eight-ounce metal container of Amoco Chrome and Metal Polish from the American Oil Company, a one-pound can of Alemite No. 33 lubricant from a division of the Steward Warner Corporation in Chicago, another one-pound can of Alemite's pure solidified oil lubricant, and a can of Peerless 4-Hour Enamel in pure green from Wilhelm Co. in Reading, Pennsylvania.* How odd addresses on these cans appeared without ZIP codes.

I tucked yellow petunias, blue lobelia, white alyssum, and ivy into the metal basket's soil. That day as he arranged each pint can upright in his bin, I'll bet he never imagined, that fifty-something years later, a single mother who not only occupied, but owned, his home would discover his cans and the rest of his trove in the very spot where he left them.

I placed the basket of plants into my wheelbarrow and watered them. In that vintage space, it became easy to recall the pungent aroma of Vovô's (Va-voo's) wine wafting up from the darkness beyond his bulkhead doors. Like Mr. Osterman, Vovô and Vovó (Va-vore) toiled at textile mills—only in North Chelmsford, about an hour north of Whitinsville. Their real passion, though, grew in their garden.

Grabbing a large terra cotta pot, and tipping it upside down on the bench, I remembered Vovô's grape arbors as if I saw them just yesterday. Those rows of simple wooden benches underneath for reaching grapes and relaxing on during family get-togethers. Standing on those benches, my cousins and I pursed our lips at the taste of Vovô's grapes every stage of the way from pea-size orange-rind-bitter to olive-size sweet and just right. At my workbench, my mind wandered into my grandparents' little yard where fruit trees and vegetables grew, and flowers wove tight paths among them all. I bumped into Vovó who was bent over, wearing her long dress and apron.

"Hi Vovó," I said.

She gazed at me, smiled, and nodded her head. Vovó didn't speak much to me. We communicated with smiles, hugs, and wet kisses on my cheeks. I plugged in my drill, tightened the bit, and bore three holes into the bottom of a pot. I tipped the pot right side up. Growing up, aunts, uncles, cousins—they were all within walking distance. Auntie Theresa, a beautiful woman of little means who always had her hair done and makeup on, sometimes a tiny crumpled piece of bloodied tissue stuck to her leg where a razor cut her that morning. She walked up the wide hilly driveway toward Dad's garage, carrying a casserole wrapped in a red-checkered towel. After losing Ma, she cared for us that way.

I placed small rocks in a pot's bottom and poured in cups-full of potting soil. I waited for our school bus at Auntie Theresa's during those years after Dorothea left and before Dad re-married. Standing in front of her window doing dishes, Auntie Theresa called me over for inspection. She took a dishcloth and scrubbed the soiled spots on my shirt, scolding me for grabbing clothes from the laundry pile. She rubbed that spot on my shirt, then watched out her window for our bus, rubbed the spot some more. As she eyed the bus coming around the corner way up the road, she sang-screamed, "The bus is coming! The bus is coming!"

Cousins popped from every corner of her small cape home.

"The bus is coming!"

Disheveled boys rumbling in her yard, cousins patting Lassie, the family's big collie chained up outside, all repeated the refrain. "The bus is coming! The bus is coming!"

Those focusing on board games on the living room floor, and me, undergoing inspection—we all dropped it and ran, lined up, and brushed ourselves off in the dirt driveway.

At my workbench I grabbed a plant, maybe another petunia, turned it upside down, and whacked it against my free palm. My cousins and I played massive games of hide n' seek at dusk, using the entire neighborhood as our stomping ground. We swam in Uncle Johnny's built-in swimming pool during summertime and huddled around his colored television, watching *Rudolph the Red-Nosed Reindeer* at Christmastime. We built wooden go-carts at Uncle Manual's. We piled into my dad's motor home for ice cream at Kimball Farms.

I tucked each plant into soil. Sprinkled water on my potted arrangement and placed it into the wheelbarrow beside the basket. My thoughts often turned to Dad's stories about growing up, his mentioning how on long walks home from church, he begged his parents for a piece of candy—just one piece. They couldn't afford it. Dorothea remembers picking blueberries with Vovó. Then Dorothea went door-to-door selling them and gave all proceeds to our grandparents. These acts of frugality and humility make my grandparents sound dirt poor. In fact though, they gave or sold most of their children a plot of land large enough for a house lot, or in my dad's case, a business.

I rolled down the top of the potting soil bag and slipped it under my bench. Lessons they laid out for me hadn't appeared until moments with my plants at that old workbench.

Using my whisk broom, I swept dirt from the bench onto a dustpan. My grandparents and other immigrants like the Ostermans sacrificed and saved in their hidey-holes, not to live day-to-day like me, but to invest in their children's futures. Like closets in my vintage home, my grandparents' closets were smaller, too. My dad and his brothers shared bedrooms. Like Mr. Osterman, my grandparents built stuff, fixed stuff, and grew stuff, all on their own property. I emptied what water remained onto the plants in my wheelbarrow and took them out to the yard where they'd grow strong and colorful. I returned, wiped off my trowel, stood it upright to dry, then shut off the lights.

Chapter 19

Catching up on some work in my front office, I heard his motorcycle putt up the driveway.

I just knew.

Slight panic in my chest, I got up that late summer day in 2014 and saw out my back window what confirmed my intuition. Henry stood beside his motorbike in a black leather jacket and unstrapped his helmet. Trying to contain my jumpy heart, I stepped outside.

"Hi," I said.

"I was around and thought I'd stop by," he said.

"It's so good to see you," I said as we embraced.

"You, too," he said.

As I invited him in, he mentioned he couldn't stay long. Had to get back on the road before dark.

We grabbed waters and headed for my patio. His hair seemed greyer. He had more wrinkles. He had a bit of a belly. Oh, but his eyes. These were the same. His soul was the same. A strand or two of bonds left between us. Like family, these were the same.

We talked for maybe an hour. All he'd been up to. All I'd been up to. Oh, he is content with another relationship now. It's not perfect, though. She'd explode if she knew he stopped by. His lover has a doctorate. They travel to Africa several times a year. They do save-the-world-type-stuff, harvesting certain difficult crops and feeding more of a certain group of people.

Oh, we lost Midnight. I've been self-employed for the last four years, doing my own medical writing now. Money comes easier. I have no lover. I will attend a *New Yorker* literary festival next month. Geoff settled into a great job as a buyer at a safety company and lives in a nearby city. Greg graduates next year, earning a degree in sport management.

The breeze blew warm as the sky turned orange. There seemed nothing left to say. All we once shared and meant to each other resided in a final gaze. We hugged goodbye. As I watched his motorbike zoom off, I remembered the night our romance died—the night I imploded on the theater steps and inside his car and demanded to "go home." Henry's inability to accept my boys set ablaze something smoldering inside me all those years. My boys are of me, as I am of my mother, as she was of hers before her. I sense all our goodness handed down through these bonds. Ma is my honesty, my empathy and forgiveness. Each boy is my joy, my hope, my fear.

His rejecting my children that night hurt. And back then, when I hurt, I wanted a safe place for my soul to return to. I wanted a grate in the floor. A Popeye egg. To gallop around the old house in my pajamas with Michael. To hide in the little alcove under it. I needed more time there to finish growing up. I was still a child.

Henry's rejecting me after the episode in his car forced the child out of me. To face that kid. Say, "What the hell's going on? Grow up."

And we all know growing up gets hard.

My desire to give the boys a good home led us to Whitinsville, drawn to an old house like the first one I ever knew before everything went wrong. In my vintage home, there came peace in restoration. Moments when I strived to preserve a flag, a stoop, a garage door, or a memory, not just for its apparent aesthetic or monetary value. But because it held a worthiness transcended by a story—of love or patriotism or culture or religion. These objects, these symbols became a collection of heritage. I served as their keeper, their storyteller; they came with a responsibility and a quiet pride. I came to discover treasures of tradition. And I found strength in my small role to ensure their survival. While traditions may break in the divisions death and dysfunction bring, I've learned they can also be rebuilt. Traditions ground me and carry me back to where I belong. They brought me home.

• • •

Punch List Item #7 – Restore garage doors and peanut brittle.

With all the care I'd given my place, it still had broken parts. Granted, most jobs, like plumbing and insulation, hid under boards and walls, contributing nothing to my home's aesthetics.

Stepping back and assessing the place, I noticed that cement apron in front of my garage, cracked like peanut brittle. Chipped garage doors. One missing a handle. Another, its bottom right corner. I had pushed these eyesores to the same part of mind where my messy mudroom and bumpy siding lived. I stopped seeing what I saw every day.

One of the garage doors no longer opened. I'd found its pulley lodged into an upside-down white ceiling paint bucket one morning. Imagined its release from the tension of a door cord slingshot across two bays until arrested by the bucket. Thankful it found its stop there and not in one of our skulls.

In times like those, I'd often debate what's better: leave things a little shabby to save money or anticipate bagging groceries as an old woman if I sprang for upgrades. I could have dug out broken pieces of cement and poured filler into those cracks. I could have just thrown another coat of paint on the doors and screwed that handle back on. While my "disposable" income still bailed out my past irresponsible spending, I had money for aesthetics. Tired of my home's wounds, I didn't want to patch up its broken places. I wanted to heal them.

In early spring 2015, I interviewed masons and garage door companies. Masons were easy to find. I settled on Leonardo for his patience and skill. I chose a combination of smooth stones in hues of foggy gray and dusty rust. Some square. Some rectangle. Garage door guys were tougher to deal with. They each carried their own product lines and I wasn't liking any. I spoke with several guys in my driveway, each at different times.

"Do you have a sample of that?" I asked one guy as we viewed a glossy brochure of carriage style doors.

164

"Sure," he said. He stuck his head in the back of his truck and fetched out a twelve- by twelve-inch piece of aluminum and passed it over.

I shook it back and forth as if shaking crumbs off paper. It wiggled like a plastic yard sale sign.

"Seems a little flimsy for a garage door, don't ya think?" I asked.

"They're all like that nowadays," he said. "We sell a lot of those."

"Don't you have anything nicer? Stronger, maybe?" I asked.

He promised returning with higher-end samples. He didn't. I called another guy.

"I'd like something nice, thicker than a cookie sheet," I explained, again standing by my garage in the driveway. "That will last a long time—maybe wood?"

"Let's take a little ride," he said. "Follow me."

He jumped into his truck. I got into my car. Followed him about a mile down Hill Street. Took a left down a long driveway. A home in pristine condition from foundation to rooftop appeared. Made of solid wood, its garage doors exuded integrity and charm.

I opened my window. "That's exactly what I want," I called over to him.

The mason came first, bringing a crew who worked from dawn to dusk. From my window, I observed a guy driving a front-end loader the size of a smart car across my driveway, digging out boulders and re-grading a sandy base. I watched how two men arranged the new stones, quickly alternating various colors in six rows as if they were setting up a game of checkers. Stone. It trumps asphalt. It trumps cement and gravel. Stone conveys all the wisdom of its past and the hope of enduring all the future holds.

A week later, three guys appeared, delivering my new garage doors and working just as long and just as hard. A choreography of bouncing up and down ladders, pulling down those old chipped doors and rusted parts, and installing new ones with their shiny rollers, door springs, cables, hinges, and electronic boxes and buttons.

Cherry wooden doors are like a woman with a fur coat, ruby lipstick, and large diamond ring on her finger. They sing to the world they were not settled for, but chosen. Together, those stones and wooden doors created the place's most elegant refinements. The splendor the house reciprocated straight into my heart as a result, extolled all its appreciation.

• • •

Later that same summer, I cleaned out a kitchen cabinet and stumbled across a plastic bag containing four disposable cameras and a couple rolls of film. I had no idea what images they held. I took them to a local drug store to see about getting them developed.

"Do you guys even still develop this stuff?"

The cashier mentioned they could send them for prints. I just had to complete some forms and they'd call me when my pictures were ready.

The day they called, I planned to jog in Uxbridge, that town next door—the one where we lived pre-divorce and where Wall Banger condo was after divorce. I agreed to grab my pictures on my way back home. As I ran toward Uxbridge town center that day, I wondered why crowds were lining up on sidewalks. As it turned out, it was for the annual baseball parade. Uxbridge kicked off its youth baseball season by parading young players in uniforms, starting from the town common and ending at the ball fields where the season's first games commenced.

I knew that parade. Racing to those same sidewalks myself year after year, I watched my boys march in their new baseball uniforms. The parade began farther along my run route, first Tee-Ball players, then Farm League, and last, Little Sluggers. As I dodged parents aiming cameras, I smiled, recalling my own boys wearing their clean uniforms back then—and remembering, too, my traditional purchase of a stain stick to combat inevitable grass and mud smears. I hadn't purchased a stain stick in years.

After my jog, I picked up the pictures and opened them in my car. In a hell of a serendipitous moment, one envelope contained pictures taken more than a decade ago just before my divorce at an Uxbridge baseball parade my sons both marched in—on a day just like that one, blue sky and all. I wondered if Ma, up there watching me, had somehow created a small coincidence, or if that was just magical thinking. It still happens now and then.

In these pictures, Geoff's about nine wearing his sky-blue baseball shirt and cap, white pants. He's tallest on the team, as they march from crosswalk to field. In one picture, he's looking at me with an expectant face as if to say, "Yep, there's my mother." In another, he's calling over to a friend, unaware of my presence. Next picture, Greg, wearing his green shirt, still has a baby face at about six and missing two front teeth. He seems surprised to see me. I shuffled to the next picture. He's watching something to his right, as are his teammates.

There's an innocence in my boys' faces in those pictures. We didn't know that day our family would soon rip apart. That the following year, they would adjust to spending time with one parent or the other, and never again with both at once. They lost their bedrooms and neighborhood. They had less time with their dad, and with me since I spent more time at work. They would endure their father's rants while I wasn't there—and honestly, mine sometimes, too, while he wasn't there. My boys wouldn't talk about their feelings regarding our coming apart. One hint could have been music I heard coming from behind Geoff's bedroom door, a Blink 182 hardcore rock song, *Stay Together for the Kids.*

When I mentioned the lyrics to Geoff, he pulled away from our conversation, as if bored. Said that all the kids listened to that song. That it was no big deal.

Still my boys' grades didn't slip. They were well behaved. They had friends and interests. We moved on pretty much in silence after divorce, just like my family moved on in silence after Ma's death amid the craziness that ensued. It's as if discussing these events aloud might resurrect all their horror. Best keep them buried, lest we rouse the demons.

Since divorce, I've attempted comparing their broken home with my own as a child struggling to absolve myself for choosing divorce. But it's impossible to compare my childhood grief with theirs and unfair to them. As a child, I tried rolling with it. Rather than reflection, there were sentiments. That God deprived me in some way. That He owed me for it. The impact of losing Ma rippled far beyond the day she chose to leave us. The loss also lives as a sentiment that I wasn't good enough for her to stay. Intellectually, I know this isn't true. That her mind dwelled in that dark place. Part of me still can't shake it. It's not a thought. It's a sense.

The remaining pictures were taken during Geoff's high school graduation party at our vintage home. His party drew droves of young people. Walking up our driveway they came, in twos, threes, some in fives.

In these pictures, teenagers sit on the lawn in shorts and t-shirts. Some girls wearing colorful headbands. Some boys wearing t-shirts featuring rock band logos across their chests. A boy stands ready, holding a fat red plastic bat. Geoff in shorts, t-shirt, and bare feet hurls a whiffle ball across our lawn; our flagpole and flag stand behind him. Another boy peeking through his long blond bangs stoops hiding behind a tree in one picture, kneeling on all fours in another, staring into the camera puckering his lips in another. Surrounded by friends, Geoff appears happy in these pictures.

Music. Their music—loud and nasty—but theirs—played that day on an outdoor stereo. They later performed a concert in our garage. The old garage I hadn't cleaned while preparing all other aspects of Geoff's party. Among rusty old parts and fixtures Mr. Osterman left behind. Among old books on shelves out there. Among empty trash cans. Right there beside that old stove we ripped out of Geoff's room, they screeched their electric guitars and pounded drums. A boy wailed into a staticky microphone—all to the discontent and patience of our kind neighbors.

Later, a large circle of kids around a campfire talked and played acoustic music while few parents who dared staying kept me company, enjoying wine on our patio deep into the night. We had so many other good times there. Heck, I threw myself a graduation party, too, when I graduated from Clark. Even my co-workers came. Dinner parties, an evening of storytelling, a local political event, my sons' sleepovers—and pancake breakfasts the following mornings.

I reluctantly set up a basketball hoop over our patio, hating mixing recreational and garden settings. However, watching Greg shoot hoops from my kitchen window and hearing the metronome of his bouncing ball brought peace in knowing he seemed safe and happy while I prepared dinner. Our front yard welcomed his dribbling and kicking a soccer ball.

The dining room hosted our quiet candlelit dinners, conducive to conversations about what's right and wrong with the world. Sitting there, too, we pored over options on collegeboard.com.

"Mom, did you say there's a degree for sport management? What would I do with that?"

And here we worked out problems arising and getting solved along the course of raising two boys.

"What do you mean you ...?"

"I'm sorry, Mom, but we were just having fun. I didn't think we'd get caught." "Mom, can I get plugs on my ears?"

"No!"

Following my tumultuous upbringing, I questioned whether I was fit for motherhood, for raising a family and keeping a home. I needed a blueprint, a frame of reference. If I searched hard enough, I would have found it in my own childhood—in the negative spaces, hidden within the calm days between neon light upheaval. The framework was there in Vovô and Vovó's gardens. In Auntie Theresa's casseroles. It appeared in Dorothea's sacrifice. In her, Andy's, and Jackie's tough love. Auntie Sister passed the plan to me every time she hugged me into her robes. It came in Dad's generosity during trips to Kimball's. It anchored in Uncle Sonny and Auntie's Jeannie's home. The lesson showed up while Eleanor recited poems and corrected my speech during the finishing school she facilitated for me. I could have discovered parts of it in the home of the family who cared for me when I ran away and in the goodness of the stranger who took me to their triple decker, not to his back seat—or trunk. It should have been apparent in Dad's hard work. Ma shared as much as she could with me in the time we had and in the time we didn't. There's a lesson in seeing a woman break, too.

That old homestead reminded me where to look. The hints of my priors' frugality, the importance they placed on spirituality, a commitment of caring for their house—a house that will always really be theirs. It conveyed that it's not about me, but my ability to protect my family and leave them better off after having known me. I kept telling myself as long as I did that, maybe we'd do okay.

Chapter 20

Having Midnight gone, both boys off and into their own lives, and more income than I ever had, I was free. To travel, to stay out until "whenever." Free from financial woes. Free from caring for or feeding anyone besides myself. Then one night I came home, a bit tipsy, I'll admit. I placed my key into the lock and opened my back door. To silence. There were no children asking whether we had anything good in the house to eat. No lover wondering where I'd been. No furry creature greeting me—someone just glad I came back.

That's why during a time when I enjoyed more independence than I'd experienced in over twenty years, I went ahead and took on more responsibility. I got a puppy. I could have adopted a rescue dog. I didn't want surprises, so I thought. I wanted a dog I could train. A creature that didn't shed. Non-allergic fur. A nice demeanor.

I searched the internet. I talked with friends and the "dog" people I knew. It all led to a poodle breeder who doesn't believe in docking tails. Imagine a standard poodle wagging a long tail. It seemed righteous in its own small way since most breeders hack off those tails only for show. He was a twelve-week-old apricot, like a red-headed human, poodle. To get my new friend, I broke up the six-hour journey in February 2015 to Colebrook, New Hampshire, a town near the Canadian border, over three days due to a snowstorm—plenty of free hours to think of a name. I settled on *Sage*, imagining him growing into a wise old dog who'd sense my moods and respond by resting his head on my lap or running to fetch a ball.

I brought a cat-sized pet carrier for transporting my new puppy home. Upon meeting him, I realized it was several sizes too small—he stood as tall as a miniature pony. I knelt. He came barreling over, jumped onto my lap, and gave me a big sloppy lick on my lips. As I wiped his drool from my mouth with a sleeve, I delighted in his greeting, considering we were in for a life-long friendship. He seemed to know that. He seemed to say, "Okay, Lady—let's go home now." And when we did, he never looked back.

Well, he is not a sage. He behaves nothing like Midnight. He is not sweet. Not gentle. He is not always loyal and not always loving. Despite having completed Puppy Kindergarten Parts One and Two, plus a private dog training lesson, Sage remains a bandit, a party boy, a running raucous. He can jump a four-foot gate in an elegant, confident bound. He will steal my undies, hand towels, phone, pens, and remote control and hold each for ransom of a treat. If I don't pay, he chomps and consumes these items. If I approach without a treat, he growls. Holds that long tail curled up high and proud, despite his misbehavior. If he were a child, he'd be drinking Jack Daniel's, smoking weed, and swearing at twelve—I just know it. However, most times, he just wants to play or cuddle. And whenever I come home, he always greets me in a generous commotion of wagging and doggy dancing.

• • •

Soon came the ten-year anniversary of Pauline's visit. Everything started to bud and bloom. I sat on a folding chair under a big white tent beside Geoff at Greg's graduation in May 2015 from Colby-Sawyer College in New London, New Hampshire. I wore a new dress I'd purchased for the occasion—black with a white trimmed scooped neck. The air felt cool. The sky blue. The sun hot. The breeze gentle.

"This moment in your life-story between chapters is so special because it's a threshold moment," said Michael Jauchen, Associate Professor of Humanities, as he began his commencement address.

Professor Jauchen delivered his talk for Greg and his classmates. Yet its message resonated with me as well. Now that both boys graduated, I felt like we made it. This time was my threshold moment, too.

While I loved my vintage home more than any other, it grew big for a single woman. In the last five years living there, I ventured upstairs maybe every couple of months—fetching Christmas decorations, putting them away, occasionally, cleaning. That's when I began to wonder about leaving. Moving my mind to make the decision was harder than moving my stuff.

When I found that place, I wanted trees and privacy. By the time I left, I was ready for the world again. I never got around to fully renovating my mudroom, kitchen, and bathrooms. That front stoop Mike and I repaired held up well, but the column bases that embraced my front door had weathered and deteriorated.

I'm a work in progress, too. Always trying to be on time, in better shape, good enough to attract the right man into my life. Striving to save enough money to survive when there's no more money coming in.

Each era of age broadens my perspective on losing Ma and all that ensued as a result. I have outlived Ma by almost twenty years. Old enough to be her mother. If at this age, I could have sat down with her the morning she decided to depart, what might she have said to me— and I to her? Maybe she'd admit feeling miserable and guilty about her misery. Trapped, and afraid. Worried over what would become of Donnie. What if he died as a child as anticipated? And if not, how could she care for him—for life? She'd probably say she's no longer the object of her husband's desire. Maybe she'd state there's nothing to look forward to anymore. Or perhaps she'd confide in me or hold back some unimaginable secret.

I would listen and listen and listen. Ask her to elaborate. To please continue. To let it all out. And when she'd shared all she could, I'd ask her to wait for me. That I'd be back tomorrow and the next day and the next day and the next one after that. There we would sit, my mother as a young suffering woman and me, at my age now, strong and listening.

After leaving my vintage home, I wondered what the next family there might assume about me as a "prior." Will they ever look at each other and say, "What's that smell?" Then rush down the basement steps to discover the poop tank pump failed? Experience an apocalyptic weekend morning—and curse me for it? Once they clean up, go over to open a window, and stumble upon the workbench, will they cherish it or want to rip it out?

I considered, too, what they might do with that old flagpole. If they keep it, will they erect a new flag to replace the faded one each year like I did? Then afterward, will they step back, look up, and swoon for a few moments in their home's patriotic history? Will they even know its history?

Maybe all that goes on there now that I'm gone will remain a mystery. For rather than leaving that place behind, I carried it with me. Echoes of my boys' voices in our hallways and from our dining room discussions. I took the peace I found at that workbench, the prudence of the hidey-hole, and the rough hands of Whitin workers in their blue chambray shirts. I brought my yard work in striving to make something better than I found it. I still see the choreographed blooms of the apple tree, the lilac, and the white bush each spring—in my mind. The flagpole outside, the flamingo tile in the shower, the chapel-shaped shelves—these too have their places in the middle of my memory's reel, which began with a grate in the floor, an alcove under a house, and an old safe behind a landscape painting.

Every other vintage home I enter will be measured against the charm of those china cabinets and arched doorways. And as some future people stand out there, admiring the stones, my spirit will float right there beside them. My vintage home's stoop, the finial atop the front room, the bow window, and wrought iron fence will create a haven in my mind to return to in meditation, driven by moments of darkness or just fatigue still inevitably to come.

Healing there, I no longer felt like someone plugged me into a high-voltage socket and left me alone to sizzle and wither away. A kind and patient guide replaced the white-hot coil living in my chest.

Instead of reacting to a series of episodic dramas, I'm viewing life now as a more plausible "whole"—the whole I observed and imagined in that house where a family who had come and gone before me remained intact. No matter how long each adventure or life itself may last, it's what and who we leave behind, *and how we leave them,* that matters. Like my immigrant priors and grandparents, I am thinking beyond myself these days, aiming toward actions that will endure past my time here. I now recognize it's not about all I can accumulate or achieve in life, but rather all I can *affect* in life.

Will I leave behind ramshackle ruins with a leaky roof, rotted wood, chipped paint, and broken steps? Or lovely paned-glass cabinetry, detailed moldings, sturdy archways, and hand-crafted floors?

This choice, this effort, I believe, has brought me finally home.

The End

Epilogue

Today, more than fifty years after losing Ma, suicide is the tenth leading cause of death in the United States. In 2019, more than 47,000 Americans committed suicide, leaving a major impact on their loved ones. It took me about thirty-five years after Ma died to seriously analyze why she may have done it. I still wonder. It took another five years to be able to talk about it—or write about it—without crying. It left a deep sadness inside of me I can never fully erase, but that I've learned to live with.

The pain of my mother's tragic departure continues rippling into our lives. Andy spent the last years of his life in anger, barely speaking to any of us. Jackie never fully recovered from drug addiction. We lost Michael from a heart attack in his forties. Dorothea and Bob dedicate their entire adult life to raising Donnie. My boys and nieces and nephews who never knew Ma must find it difficult to understand why we stare at each other and shake our lowered heads without saying a word sometimes.

There is no one cause for suicide, but there are warning signals to watch for. A full list of warning signals resides at afsp.org. Some signals include people talking about killing themselves and feeling trapped and hopeless. They may increase drug and alcohol use, withdraw, give away valuables, or sleep too much or too little. They may have depression, anxiety, anger, or experience shame or humiliation. If you know someone having a rough time:

- Talk to them in private.
- Listen to their story.

- Tell them you care.
- Ask if they are thinking about suicide.
- Encourage them to seek treatment or to contact their doctor or therapist.
- Avoid debating the value of life, minimizing their problems, or giving advice.

If you know someone who is thinking about committing suicide:
- Take them seriously.
- Stay with them or call for emergency help (police) to go to them.
- Help them remove lethal means.
- Call the National Suicide Prevention Lifeline: 1-800-273-8255.
- Tell them they can text TALK to 741741 to text with a trained crisis counselor from the Crisis Text Line for free.
- Escort them to mental health services or an emergency room.

If you are thinking about suicide, please seek help from an emergency room or mental health services right away. Believe me when I say you will be missed more and for longer than you could ever imagine.

Acknowledgements

I thank the Osterman family for sanctioning this endeavor, especially Vincent who was kind enough to share some memories of his grandparents and their home. I thank Derek Zeyl, former pastor of the Pleasant Street Christian Reformed Church, Whitinsville, Massachusetts, who arranged a coffee hour so I could speak with parishioners who shared their faith, stories about the Dutch, and their memories of the Ostermans. Your stories touched my heart and helped inform my understanding of earlier days in Whitinsville, and what a treasured past you shared growing up there. I thank Jim and Jean Nydam for inviting me into your home and sharing with me your stories and understanding of the Dutch people's immigration to Whitinsville.

A very warm and special thanks to my good friend Kenneth Warchol, who is likely the most knowledgeable person on the history of Whitinsville. Your knowledge about the town's history, combined with your wisdom as an educator breathed life into my understanding of its origins and transformations.

Thank you to Brown University's Writer's Symposium and Ed Hardy for the instruction and support you provided as I began this journey. Warm appreciation to Grub Street-Boston instructors for your support and wisdom. I thank Joanne Wyckoff for your class on *Finding Your Book* and Steve Almond for your classes on making scenes and storytelling. You are so wise. I thank Ethan Gilsdorf for teaching about submissions, Amy Yelin for your skill in the literary essay, Alexandria Marzano-Lesnevich for your insights into writing the personal essay, all of my classmates for sharing your comments, insights, and knowledge,

Eve Bridburg for everything you have done to pull this extraordinary organization together. I love you all. You are my people.

Thank you to the Fine Arts Work Center in Provincetown for your thoughtful classes and overall programming. Brian Turner, thank you for the insightful experience you provided in our summer workshop and for encouraging me with your imaginative instruction. To Marion Roach Smith, you are brilliant. A heartful of thanks to you for your review and critique of my early manuscript. Your comments spawned new light and provided just the right inspiration to keep going.

Thank you so much to Shanna McNair and Scott Wolven for The Writer's Hotel (TWH) experience, which provided me the reality and the courage to step up and face my childhood, one word at a time. I thank you also for your many edits and insights. To Saïd Sayrafiezadeh, a heartfelt thanks for your patience and wisdom during our spring 2017 session at TWH.

Kate Baldwin, thank you for saving me from myself by identifying my typos and infelicities.

A special thanks to Reagan Rothe, creator of Black Rose Writing (BRW), for your support and acceptance of this work. Thank you so much to David King for your expert design and everyone else on the BRW team for your dedication to getting this book out there.

To the Baker Library staff at Harvard University, I am in awe at how you maintain the integrity of the Whitin mill archives with such diligence. I also express gratitude to those who made the good decision to entrust the mill's archives into the capable hands of the Baker Library.

Thank you to my nephew, Todd Chase, who kindly instructed me on the correct technical vernacular to describe tow truck lights.

A warm thanks to Geoff, my big boy, who patiently listened to excerpts, set me straight on some crucial facts, and expressed heartfelt concern over the tender spots. Great appreciation to Greg, my little boy, who also patiently listened to excerpts and offered wise counsel. And to Ally, my sweet daughter-in-law, thank you for being the first to bring a quote from this book to life on the lovely sign you created. With you kids, I will always be truly at home

In memory of Eleanor, you were a kind woman and a good mother—and you got way more than you bargained for from the daughter you always wanted.

I thank my sister Dorothea and her husband Bob for your selfless and lifelong devotion to us kids, and especially for your loving and unrelenting care of Donnie.

Bibliography

National down syndrome society. What is Down Syndrome? Accessed March 2, 2021. https://www.ndss.org/about-down-syndrome/down-syndrome/

Navin, T The Whitin Machine Works Since 1831, A Textile Machinery Company in an Industrial Village. 1950. Harvard University Press, Cambridge, Massachusetts.

Hurley, M. A Way of Life, Not Just a Place. Circa 1984. Blackstone Valley Tribune.

Marshall-Griffin, M A Woman Recalls Life in the New Village. Circa 1984. Blackstone Valley Tribune.

King, P Whitinsville a Model Village, Place Where Capitalism, Feudalism, Communism Go Hand in Hand—Ruled by Whitin-Lasell Dynasty. June 2, 1929. Boston Sunday Post.

Hurley, M Navin; The Man Who Wrote the Book. Circa 1983. The Blackstone Valley Tribune.

Galema, A Whitinsville, Massachusetts. ORIGINS. Historical Magazine of The Archives – The Hekman Library Calvin College and Theological Seminary. Volume XII, November 2, 1994.

Semon, C Uxbridge man restores steam engines made during WWII. November 15, 2013. Worcester Telegram & Gazette.

Lyons, LM 1,000 Families in the Bay State Show Us How to Use Our Land. Boston Daily Globe. January 19, 1926.

Weather Underground. Weather History for KBED March 1968. Accessed July 29, 2017. https://www.wunderground.com/history/airport/KBED/1968/3/21/Dail yHistory.html?req_city=Chelmsford&req_state=MA&req_statename= Massachusetts&reqdb.zip=01824&reqdb.magic=1&reqdb.wmo=9999 9.

Buynoski, M. MadSci[SM] Network. July 29, 2017. [Email] Could a frozen pond remain frozen after 5 days of temps above 41 deg F?

Hutchens, B, Kearney, J Risk Factors for Postpartum Depression: An Umbrella Review. Journal of Midwifery & Women's Health. February 2020. https://onlinelibrary.wiley.com/doi/epdf/10.1111/jmwh.13067

American Foundation for Suicide Prevention. Accessed March 3, 2021. https://afsp.org/suicide-statistics

Note from the Author

Word-of-mouth is crucial for any author to succeed. If you enjoyed *Home, My Story of House and Personal Restoration*, please leave a review online—anywhere you are able. Even if it's just a sentence or two. I would be thrilled to hear your thoughts and would very much appreciate it.

Thanks!
M.G. Barlow

We hope you enjoyed reading this title from:

Subscribe to our mailing list – *The Rosevine* – and receive
FREE books, daily deals, and stay current with news about
upcoming releases and our hottest authors.
Scan the QR code below to sign up.

Already a subscriber? Please accept a sincere thank you for
being a fan of Black Rose Writing authors.

CPSIA information can be obtained
at www.ICGtesting.com
Printed in the USA
FSHW022145150222
88247FS

9 781684 337767